Basic Vocabulary *in use*

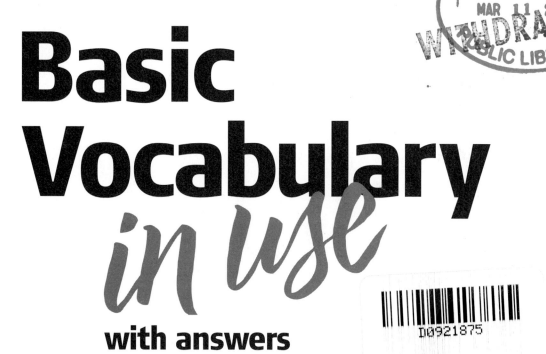

with answers

Michael McCarthy
Felicity O'Dell
with Ellen Shaw

CAMBRIDGE UNIVERSITY PRESS
Cambridge, New York, Melbourne, Madrid, Cape Town, Singapore, São Paulo, Delhi

Cambridge University Press
32 Avenue of the Americas, New York, NY 10013–2473, USA

www.cambridge.org
Information on this title: www.cambridge.org/9780521788656

First published 2001
14th printing 2008

Printed in Hong Kong, China, by Golden Cup Company Limited

A catalog record for this publication is available from the British Library

Library of Congress Cataloging in Publication Data
McCarthy, Michael
Basic vocabulary in use : reference and practice for students of North American English
/Michael McCarthy, Felicity O'Dell, with Ellen Shaw.
p. cm.
Includes index.
ISBN 978-0-521-78865-6 (pbk. : with answers) —ISBN 978-0-521-78864-9 (pbk. : without answers)
1. Vocabulary—Problems, exercises, etc. 2. English language—Textbooks for foreign
speakers. I. O'Dell, Felicity, 1947— II. Shaw, Ellen.
PE1449.M393   2001
428.1—dc21

00-052942

ISBN 978-0-521-78864-9 Student's Book without answers
ISBN 978-0-521-78865-6 Student's Book with answers

Art direction, book design, and layout services: GTS Graphics, Los Angeles, CA
Illustrations: Kathy Baxendale, Nora Koerber, Amanda Macphail, Scot Ritchie, Anne Stanley,
and Gary Wing.

Contents

The headphones symbol ⌒ means that example sentences from this unit are on the audio CD that comes with this book.

Acknowledgments

We wish to thank Laura MacGregor, Sophia University, Tokyo, Japan; Cheryl Zimmerman, ESL Program Coordinator, California State University–Fullerton; and Eliane Zamboni, Centro de Ensino de Línguas, São Paulo, Brazil, whose comments were so helpful in improving the book as it developed. We also wish to thank Janaka Williams of Cambridge University Press, whose expert scrutiny contributed further to making the book a better one. Also at Cambridge University Press, David Bohlke's editorial advice was invaluable, and Paul Heacock helped get the book finished. But, above all, the authors are indebted to our American adapter, Ellen Shaw, who not only made sure the text was faithful to American English usage, but who made numerous suggestions for improving the content and the exercises. Without Ellen's collaboration, we would not be publishing this American edition.

We would like to thank those who helped in the making of *English Vocabulary in Use–Elementary*, the British English book on which this is based: Gillian Lazar, Geraldine Mark, and Stuart Redman for their invaluable reports on the initial manuscript. We are also grateful to the students and staff at various institutions who assisted in piloting the material in different parts of the world: Hülya Akgün, Özel Gökdil Lisesi, Istanbul, Turkey; Monika Barczyk, Sosnowiec, Poland; Anna Cerna, The Bell School, Prague, Czech Republic; Leigh Fergus, Paris, France; Sharon Hartle, Verona, Italy; Gary Hicks and David Parry, Embassy Language and Training Centre, Hove, England; Grazyna Kanska, Warsaw, Poland; Stephanie Lott, St. John's–Bell Language Centre, Bangkok, Thailand; Elena Marinina, Moscow State University, Moscow, Russia; Dr. Miroslawa Modrzewska, Gdansk, Poland; Dr. Ramzy Radwan, Cairo, Egypt; M. G. Rogers, English One, Seville, Spain; Margot Teschendorf, Melbourne, Australia.

Many thanks are due Nóirín Burke of Cambridge University Press, who guided this book through the editorial process. She set the deadlines that motivated us to get the book done, and chased us when we lagged behind. Geraldine Mark, as usual, proved to be the most professional of editors when the manuscript passed into her hands and made many useful comments that have improved the book. Our domestic partners must always get a special thank you for being so tolerant of the long hours we spend away from them in the company of our computer keyboards. Whatever faults and shortcomings remain in the book must be laid entirely at our door.

Michael McCarthy

Felicity O'Dell

Cambridge, December 2000

To the Student

This book has been written to help you learn new vocabulary. You already know hundreds of English words, but to speak and write English in normal situations you need to know at least 1,000–2,000 words. In this book, there are around 1,250 new words and phrases for you to learn. You will find them on the left-hand page of each unit. Every new word or phrase is used in a sentence, or in a conversation, or has a picture with it, or has some explanation of what it means. On the right-hand page there are exercises and other activities to help you practice using the words and to help you to remember them. The book has been written so that you can use it yourself, without a teacher. You can do the units in any order you like, but we believe it is a good idea if you do Units 1 and 2 first, as they will help you to work with the rest of the book in the best possible way.

New vocabulary for each topic is on the left-hand page. First of all, the vocabulary is divided into sections (A, B, C, etc.) with simple, clear titles. New words and phrases [groups of words] are usually printed in **bold type** [dark letters] and explained in one of these ways:

- A short definition [explanation of the meaning]. The definition comes after the word or at the end of the phrase or sentence; it is in brackets [ ]: **unemployed** [without a job]; **make up your mind** [make a decision].

- An example, usually with "e.g.," which means "for example": **Country** can mean a nation (e.g., Brazil, Japan, Italy).

- A slash (/) is often used to show that two words or phrases have similar meanings:
  Do you ever **have trouble / have problems** understanding English? [have difficulty]
  Sometimes slashes show different words or phrases that you can use in the same position in a sentence. The words don't always mean the same thing:
  Have a nice day/evening/weekend. [We say this when we say good-bye.]

- Parentheses ( ) around a word shows that you can use it or not use it:
  The movie **made me (feel) sad** = The movie made me sad. OR
  The movie made me feel sad.

- The word *not* shows that a phrase is wrong. It often points to common student errors:
  She does her homework every evening. (*not* She ~~makes~~ her homework every evening.)

- A picture or diagram. This is the clearest way to illustrate a large number of nouns and verbs.

- For many new words, sentence examples give a situation that helps you understand the meaning:

My friend called me stupid. It **made me angry.**
She went away for three days. She **came back** yesterday. [She is here again.]
I hated my sister when I was young, but now we **get along** very well.

There is an answer key at the back of the book. This not only gives correct answers to exercises with "right" or "wrong" solutions, but also possible answers and suggested answers for exercises that do not have "right" or "wrong" solutions.

The index at the end of the book has all the important words and phrases from the left-hand pages. The index also tells you how to pronounce words. There is a table of pronunciation symbols on page 125 to help you understand the pronunciation.

You should also have a dictionary with you when you use the book. You may want to check the meaning of something, or find a word in your own language to help you remember the English word. Sometimes, you will also need a dictionary for the exercises; we tell you when this is so.

To learn a lot of vocabulary, you have to do two things:

1. Study each unit of the book carefully and do all the exercises. Check your answers in the answer key. Repeat the units after a month, and then again after three months, and see how much you have learned and how much you have forgotten. Repeating work is very important.

2. Develop ways of your own to study and learn new words and phrases which are not in this book. For example, every time you see or hear an interesting phrase, write it in a notebook, and write who said it or wrote it, and in what situation, as well as what it means. Here is an interesting example:

ready: *(man at the door of a theater, to all the people waiting)* "Have your tickets ready please!" = have your ticket in your hand.

Making notes of the situations words are used in will help you to remember them and to use them at the right moment.

We hope you like this book. When you have finished it, you can go to the next book in the series, *Vocabulary in Use: Intermediate,* and after that, to the higher level, *Vocabulary in Use: Upper Intermediate.*

To the Teacher

This book can be used in class or as a self-study book. It is intended to take learners from a very basic level of vocabulary to a level where they can use around 2,000 words and phrases. The vocabulary has been chosen for its usefulness in everyday situations, and the authors consulted a written and spoken corpus of present-day English to help them decide on the words and phrases to be included. The new vocabulary (on average 20–25 items per unit) is presented with illustrations and explanations on the left-hand page, and there are exercises and activities on the right-hand page. There is an index with pronunciation for all the key vocabulary, a table of phonetic symbols, and an answer key at the end of this book.

The book focuses not just on single words, but on useful phrases and collocations. For example, difficult teaching points such as the difference between **do** and **make** are dealt with through collocation (we **do** our homework, but we **make** mistakes), and useful phrases (e.g., **come over**, in the unit on **come**) are presented.

The book is organized around everyday topics, but also has units devoted to core verbs such as **get** and **bring/take**, as well as units concerned with ways of learning vocabulary. Typical errors are indicated where appropriate, and the most typical meanings and uses are focused on for each key item. The units in the book can be used in any order you like, but we would advise doing the initial units on learning vocabulary (Units 1 and 2) first, as these lay the foundations for the rest of the book.

The right-hand pages offer a variety of different types of activities, some traditional ones such as fill-in-the-blanks, but also more open-ended ones and personalized activities which enable learners to talk about their own lives. Although the activities and exercises are designed for self-study, they can be easily adapted for pair work, group work, or whole-class activities in the usual way.

When learners have worked through a group of units, it is a good idea to repeat some of the work (for example, the exercises) and to expand on the meaning and use of key words and phrases by extra discussion in class, and find other examples of the key items in other texts and situations. This can be done at intervals of one to three months after first working on a unit. This is important, since it is usually the case that a learner needs five to seven exposures to a word or phrase before they can really know it, and no single book can do enough to ensure that words are always learned first time.

When your students have finished all the units in this book, they will be ready to move on to the two higher level books in this series: *Vocabulary in Use: Intermediate* by Stuart Redman, and after that, to the higher level, *Vocabulary in Use: Upper Intermediate*, by the same authors as this book.

We hope you enjoy using the book.

Talking about language

Language words

Grammar word	Meaning	Example	In your language
noun	a person, place, or thing	Mary, China, pen	
verb	something we do	do, read, write	
adjective	describes a noun	good, bad, happy, long	
adverb	describes a verb	slowly, badly	
preposition	use it before a noun or pronoun	in, on, by, at, through	
singular	one noun	book, house, child	
plural	more than one noun	books, houses, children	
phrase	a group of words (*not* a complete sentence)	in a house, at home, an old man	
sentence	an idea that begins with a (capital letter) and ends with a (period); a sentence usually has a subject and a verb.	(T)he man went into the room and closed the door.	
paragraph	one or more sentences about the same topic, beginning on a new line	This book has 60 units. Each unit has 2 pages.	
question	a group of words that begin with a (capital letter) and end with a (question mark)	(W)hat time is it? Do you speak Spanish(?)	

Instructions used in this book

1. Match the words on the left with the words on the right. Draw lines.
   orange ——— ice cream
   chocolate ——— juice
2. Fill in the blank.
   Maria is ......*at*...... home today.
3. Correct the mistakes.
   Maria is ~~in~~ home today. ...*Maria is at home today.*....
4. Complete the sentence about yourself.
   I go to work by ....*bus*..... .
5. Add another example.
   cat, dog, horse, ...*cow*.....

Exercises

1.1 Write the grammar words in A on page 4 in your own language.

1.2 Write these words in the correct column.

shirt speak bad car banana have
write new woman old sad eat

Noun	Verb	Adjective
shirt		

1.3 Write four prepositions.

...*of,* ..in,.the.,.an.,.a...

1.4 Are these phrases, sentences, or questions?

1. in the park ....*phrase*..........
2. Do you speak English? ....*question*......
3. a black cat .....*phrase*........
4. She's writing a book. ....*sentences*........
5. What's your name? ...*question*..........
6. I like English. .....*sentence*......

man
men

1.5 Answer these questions.

1. What is the plural of **book**? ....*books*........
2. What is the singular of **women**? ...*woman*..........
3. Is **from** a verb? .....*No, it isn't. from is a preposition*✗
4. Is **cat** an adjective? *No, it isn't. it is a Noun*
5. Is "**Jane loves Harry.**" a phrase? ..*No, it isn't. it is a Sentence*

1.6 Follow these instructions.

1. Fill in the blank. What ....*is*.... your name?
2. Add another example of a color. black, green, blue ,..*white*.., ..*yellow, grey, brown*
3. Correct the mistakes. speek, inglish *speak , English.*
4. Match the verbs on the left with the nouns on the right. Draw lines.

   make ———— homework
   do ——✗—— a shower
   take ——✗— a mistake

   made

5

UNIT 2 Learning strategies

Tip: Keep a vocabulary notebook. Write the words you learn from this book in your notebook. Use a good dictionary. Ask your teacher to recommend one. You will need it for some exercises in this book.

A   Write down words that go together (collocations).

You **do the exercises** in this book. Sometimes, you **make mistakes** in English. In your vocabulary notebook, write: **do an exercise** and **make a mistake**.

When words are used together like this, we call it a **collocation**.

You go **by train**, but **on foot** [walking].	preposition + noun
Some people are **good at** languages. (*not* good ~~in~~)	adjective + preposition
I saw a very **tall man**. (*not* ~~high~~ man)	adjective + noun

Tip: Always write down collocations when you learn a new word.

B   Learn words in families.

Word family	*Some words in the family*
temperature	hot, warm, cool, cold
travel	ticket, passport, suitcase

Tip: Make a page for every different word family in your vocabulary notebook.

C   Pictures and diagrams

Draw pictures in your notebook to help remember words.
For example: **car**

Draw diagrams like this one. Add more words as you learn them.

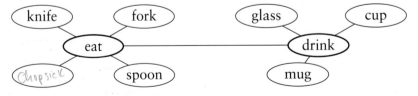

Tip: When you can, use pictures and diagrams.
One more tip: Look at the words you have written down again and again!

Exercises

2.1 Look at Unit 3. How many more collocations for *have* can you write in your vocabulary notebook?

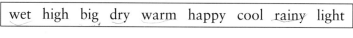

.....*have a party, have lunch,*....... *have breakfast,.......have a cup of tea.*.....

2.2 Which words can go with *weather*? Use a dictionary.

wet high big dry warm happy cool rainy light

wet

dry
warm	— weather
cool
rainy

2.3 There are two word families here. Complete the chart with the word families and examples from the box. Use a dictionary.

school bread teacher milk notebook exam water salad student rice

Name of word family	Words in family
education	school, teacher, notebook, exam student
food	**bread**, milk , water, salad, rice

2.4 Draw simple pictures to help you remember these words.

Example: to cry

1. a plane **lands**
2. **sunny weather**
3. **under** the table

2.5 Write words in the empty circles.

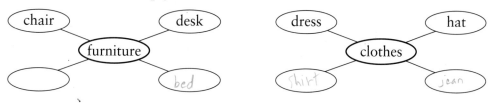

Tip: Now make sure you have started a vocabulary notebook before you do the other units in this book.

UNIT 3 — Have

A — Have

Have often means to own or possess.

> I **have** a computer.
> We **have** a small house.
> I **don't have** enough money to buy a car.

B — What can you *have*?

You can . . .

> **have** breakfast.
> **have** a party.
> **have** a class.
> **have** a cup of coffee/tea.
> **have** a cold (when you're sick).

C — Other things you can *have*

Example	Other things
breakfast	dinner lunch a meal something to eat
a party	a meeting a date [a social/romantic meeting] a good time an argument
a class	homework an exam an appointment (with the dentist)
a cup of coffee/tea	something to drink a drink a snack [a little food between meals]
a cold	the flu a headache a broken arm a sore throat

D — Expressions with *have*

> I'm going to **have my hair cut.** [Someone is going to cut my hair.]
> Good-bye! **Have a good trip!** [when someone is going away]
> I **have a brother and two sisters.**
> She's going to **have a baby** next month. [give birth]
> I want to learn to ski, but I **don't have the time.**
> Do you ever **have trouble / have problems** understanding English? [difficulty]

E — Have to = must

Use **have to** when something is necessary and you have no choice.

> The museum isn't free. You **have to** pay $10 to get in.
> She **has to** take an exam at the end of the course.

MUSEUM
entrance $10

Use **don't have to** when something is not necessary or not required.

> I **don't have to** work on Saturdays.
> We **don't have to** go to the party if you don't want to.

F — Have got / have got to (speaking/informal) = *have / have to*

> **I've got** a bad cold – Stay away!
> **Have you got** a minute? I need to talk to you.
> **I've got to run!** [I have to go right now] See you later!

Exercises

3.1   Fill in the blanks. Use words from B, C, and D on page 8.

1. I never have a big ..*breakfast*.. in the morning.
2. I have an .... with the doctor at 1 o'clock.
3. I had an .... yesterday, so I had to study all last week.
4. Mike is having a .... on Saturday night. Are you going?
5. I want to take a vacation this summer, but I don't have the ....
   I'm too busy.
6. I have a terrible .... I keep sneezing. Atchoo!
7. I had a .... with Maria last night. We went out to dinner and a movie.
8. Keiko is going to have a .... She thinks it'll be a girl.

3.2   Answer the questions about yourself.

1. Do you have any brothers or sisters? If yes, how many?
2. Which days do you have to go to class?
3. What do you usually have for lunch?
4. On weekends do you have to get up early in the morning?
5. Do you ever have arguments with your friends?
6. Is there anything you have at home that you don't need?
7. How often do you have your hair cut?
8. Do you ever have trouble understanding English?

3.3   Do the crossword puzzle.

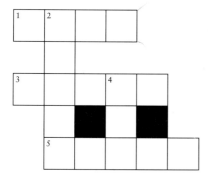

Across
1. You can have one in a restaurant.
3. Some people like to have one on New Year's Eve.
5. You have this between meals.

Down
2. You have these at school.
4. If you don't want coffee, you can have ....

3.4   What do you say when . . .

1. someone is thirsty?   Why don't you have .... ?
2. someone is going away on vacation?   Bye! Have a .... !
3. you want to talk to someone but don't know if he or she has time?
   Have you got a .... ?

UNIT 4 *Go*

A   **Go**

Go means to move from one place to another.
> I **go** to work by bus. My brother **goes** by car.
> We **went** to Mexico last summer.
> Let's **go** to the movies tonight.

Is this bus **going** downtown?

Where **does** this road **go**?

B   **Go + prepositions**

Kim **went in(to)** her room.

Kanako **went out of** the house.

Paulo **went up** the stairs slowly.

Ann **went down** the stairs quickly.

C   **Go + -ing for activities**

Use **go** with **-ing** for certain activities.

I hate **going shopping**.

I usually **go swimming** in the morning.

Let's **go dancing**.

Do you **go sightseeing** when you are on vacation?

Ana **goes skiing** in the winter.

Bob is **going fishing** today.

D   **Future plans with *be going to***

On Saturday John **is going to visit** his aunt. On Sunday we **are going to stay** at home. On Monday I'**m going to meet** Sam for lunch.

Exercises

4.1 Where are they going? Follow the lines.

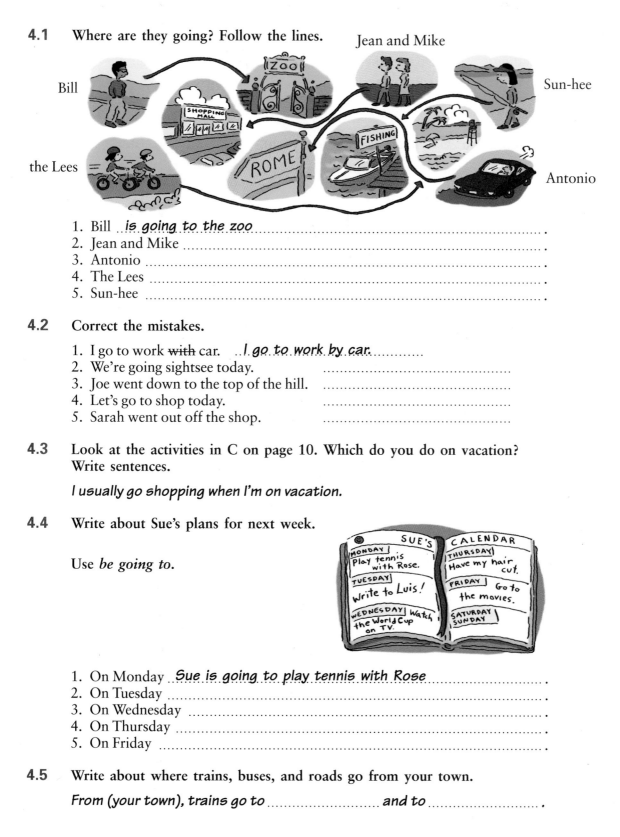

Bill

Jean and Mike

Sun-hee

the Lees

Antonio

1. Bill *is going to the zoo* ....
2. Jean and Mike ....
3. Antonio ....
4. The Lees ....
5. Sun-hee ....

4.2 Correct the mistakes.

1. I go to work ~~with~~ car.   *I go to work by car.* ....
2. We're going sightsee today. ....
3. Joe went down to the top of the hill. ....
4. Let's go to shop today. ....
5. Sarah went out off the shop. ....

4.3 Look at the activities in C on page 10. Which do you do on vacation? Write sentences.

I usually go shopping when I'm on vacation.

4.4 Write about Sue's plans for next week.

Use *be going to*.

1. On Monday *Sue is going to play tennis with Rose* ....
2. On Tuesday ....
3. On Wednesday ....
4. On Thursday ....
5. On Friday ....

4.5 Write about where trains, buses, and roads go from your town.

From (your town), trains go to .... *and to* ....

11

UNIT 5 *Do*

A *Do* as auxiliary

Questions	Do you like tennis?	Did they like the movie?
Short answers	Yes, I **do**.	Yes, they **did**.
	So **does** Mari.	So **did** I.
Negatives	He **doesn't play** well.	Bob **didn't see** it.

B What are you *doing*? (*Do* as a general verb)

What are the people in the picture **doing**?
  They're dancing.

What do you **do** to relax?
  I listen to music.

Don't **do** that, Tommy.

C What *do* you *do*? [What is your job?]

What **do** you **do**? [What is your job?]
  I'm a student. *or* I'm a teacher. *or* I'm an engineer.
What **does** your wife **do**? [What is your wife's job?]
  She's a sales rep. *or* She's a secretary. *or* She's a doctor.

D *Do* + task

do the housework [clean the home]
do the laundry [wash clothes]
do the dishes [wash dishes]
do the cooking
do exercises
do business with

Did you **do the dishes** this morning?
  No, I'm going to **do** them later.
Our company **does a lot of business with** Canada.
You always **do a good job**.

Tip: Write down expressions with **do** that you find when you are reading in English.

(See Unit 6 for differences between **do** and **make**.)

Exercises

5.1   Write questions and answers about the people in the picture.

1. (the boy) .....*What is the boy doing? He's eating ice cream.*.................
2. (the woman)...
3. (the girls)...
4. (the man in the house) ....
5. (the dog) ....

5.2   Write questions and answers about the jobs of the people in the pictures.

1. Lara Brown   2. Bill Atkins   3. Maria Santos   4. Ted and Kumiko

1. .....*What does Lara Brown do? She's a secretary.*...........................
2. ....
3. ....
4. ....

5.3   Write questions about what the people in exercise 5.2 did this morning. Answer the questions using the phrases in the box.

| meet with five patients   teach three lessons   write essays   go to a meeting |

1. .....*What did Lara Brown do? She went to a meeting.*........................
2. ....
3. ....
4. ....

5.4   Look at the *do* expressions in D on page 12. Write sentences about you or your family and these activities.

I usually do the cooking at home, but I never do the laundry.

UNIT 6 *Make*

A *Make . . . (food and drinks)*

to **make coffee**

to **make dinner /
make a meal**

I'll **make** some **tea/soup**.
I **make breakfast/lunch/dinner** every day.

B *Make a . . .*

She's **making a phone
call / a telephone call.**

He's **making a
photocopy.**

She's **making a
video / a movie.**

C **Don't *make* mistakes with *make*!**

Can I say . . . ?	yes/no	Correction
I **made** a mistake in the exercise.	✓	
I have to ~~make~~ my homework.	✗	I have to **do** my homework.
I have to ~~make~~ an exam next week.	✗	I have to **take** an exam next week.
Do you want to stay or go? You have to **make** a decision. [decide]	✓	
I have to **make** an appointment with the doctor/dentist/hairdresser. [fix a time to see that person]	✓	
I'd like to ~~make~~ a photo of you.	✗	I'd like to **take** a photo of you.
After dinner I'll ~~make~~ the dishes.	✗	After dinner I'll **do** the dishes.

D **It *makes* me (feel) . . .**

Taking planes always **makes me (feel)** nervous.
My friend called me stupid. It **made me (feel)** angry.
That movie **made me (feel)** sad.

Exercises

6.1 Fill in the blanks with *make* or *do*.

1. I always ...*make*... mistakes when I speak English.
2. Let's go to bed now. We can .... the dishes in the morning.
3. I'm going to .... some coffee. Would you like a cup?
4. The children always .... a lot of phone calls in the evening.
5. If I .... my homework every day, my English will improve.

6.2 Complete the sentences with *make(s) me (feel)* or *made me (feel)*.

1. That movie .... sad.
2. Exams at school always .... nervous.
3. The salesclerk wasn't very nice to me; it .... angry.

6.3 What are these people doing? Complete the sentences with *make*.

1. She's .... 3. He's ....

2. She's .... 4. They're ....

6.4 Correct the mistakes.

1. I have to ~~make~~ my homework.   *I have to do my homework.*
2. Can I make a photo of you?
3. He's 35, but he never makes his own laundry. He takes his dirty clothes to his mother's.
4. I have to take an appointment with the dentist.
5. Do students have to make an exam at the end of their English course?
6. Yes or no? We have to do a decision today.

Come

A Come and go are different.

HERE ←——— come   HERE ——— go ——→ THERE

B Come in and come out

You can say **"Come in!"** when someone knocks at the door of a room.
Then the person who knocked **comes into** the room.

You put your money in, and the ticket **comes out of** the machine.

C Come back and come home

Come back means "return to *this place here*."
  She went away for three days. She **came back** yesterday. [She is here again.]

We often use **come back** with **from**.
  They **came back from** Italy yesterday.

Come home is similar. "Home" is "here" for the person speaking.
  MOTHER TO SON (*on the telephone*):
  Don't stay out too late. **Come home** early.

D Other expressions with come

A: What country do you **come from**? / Where do you **come from**?
B: **I'm from** Mexico. *or* I **come from** Mexico. *or* **I'm** Mexican.
  (*not* I'm come from Mexico.)

Can I **come over** and see you tonight? [visit someone]

A: I can't go with you.
B: **How come?** [Why is that?]

Tip: Write down any prepositions you find with **come** every time you see them.

Exercises

7.1 **Fill in the blanks.**

1. I put money in, but the ticket didn't come ..*out of*.. the machine.
2. A: I'm going to Hawaii tomorrow.
   B: Oh! When are you coming ....?
   A: In two weeks.
3. A: Where do you come ....?
   B: I'm Brazilian.
4. A: I'll be home late tonight.
   B: Oh, really? .... come?
   A: Because I have to work late.
5. The children come .... from school at 4 o'clock.

7.2 **Answer these questions about *yourself*.**

1. What time do you come home every day?
2. What country (or city or town) do you come from?
3. What is the first thing you do when you come into your classroom?

7.3 **What do you think these people are saying?**

We're going to have a barbecue at home this weekend. Would you like to . . . ?

1. ....   2. ....

7.4 **Fill in the blanks using *come* in the correct form.**

1. We .... back from Singapore last night.
2. Where does she .... from?
3. He .... here every Tuesday.
4. Are you .... to the school party tonight?
5. I put a dollar into the machine, and a can of soda .... out.

7.5 **Look up these verbs in a dictionary. Write down only *one* meaning for each verb, even if you find more than one meaning.**

1. come across   2. come on   3. come up

7.6 After a week, cover the verbs in 7.5, look at your notes, and see if you can remember the verbs.

Take

A   *Take* with time (it + takes + person + time)

It **takes** Alan 20 minutes to get to work.
Alan's house → 20 minutes → Alan's office

It **takes** Maria 45 minutes to get to work.
Maria's apartment → 45 minutes → Maria's office

home   work

I go to school/class every day. It **takes** me 30 minutes.
I do homework every day. It **took** me two hours yesterday.

A: **How long does it take** to get to the airport?
B: An hour by taxi.

B   *Take* with courses, exams, etc.

Are you **taking** an English course? Yes.
Do you have to **take** an exam?
    Yes, at the end of the course.
I want to **take** Italian lessons.

C   *Take* with bus, train, etc.

How do you get to work?
    I **take** the bus.

In New York you can **take** the subway
to the World Trade Center.

A: How does Nick get to work?
B: He **takes** the train.

D   *Take* something with you

Are you going out? **Take** an
umbrella. It's raining.

Are you going to the beach? **Take**
some water with you.

I'm sorry, but you can't **take**
your camera into the museum.

Useful expression: Can I **take a photograph/photo/picture** here?

Tip: Make a page in your notebook for **take** and put in new words that go
with it when you see them (e.g., **take** a picture, **take** a chance, **take**
medicine).

Exercises

8.1 Complete the sentences about *yourself*.

1. It .... me .... minutes to get to school/class.
2. It takes me .... minutes/hours to go from .... to ....
3. .... takes me .... to do one unit of this book.

8.2 Complete the sentences using *take/took* and an expression from the box.

a course   your driving test   an exam

1. At the end of the course, you have to ....
2. I wanted to learn French, so I ....
3. In some countries, when you are 17, you can ....

8.3 Look at the pictures. Answer the questions using *take*.

1. How does Mariko go to work?
   She ....

3. How does Jack go to school?
   He ....

2. How do I get to the airport?
   You ....

4. How do Pedro and Ana get home every day?
   They ....

8.4 What do you take with you when . . .

1. you want to take photographs? ...*I take a camera.*...

2. it's raining?

3. you travel to another country?

4. you go to your English class?

8.5 How long did it take you to do this unit?

UNIT 9 *Bring*

A Bring *and* take

bring = from *there* to *here*
[toward you]
take = from *here* to *there*
[away from you]

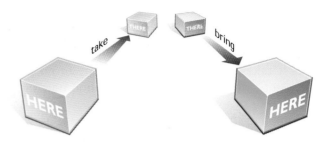

Are you going to school? **Take** your books. (from *here* to the school)
TEACHER: Remember to **bring** your books to school tomorrow. (The school is
    here.)

Please **take** this form to the secretary. (The secretary is *there*.)

Are you going to the kitchen? Can you **bring** me a glass of water?
(from the kitchen *to here*)

B Bring *somebody something*

A: I **brought** you some fruit.   When she returns from a trip,
B: Oh, thank you!   she always **brings** me a gift.

C Bring *something* back

It's raining. You can **take** my umbrella and
bring it **back** tomorrow.

TOM: This magazine is really interesting.
ANN: You can **take** it with you and read it.
TOM: Thanks. I'll **bring** it **back** on Friday.
ANN: OK. No problem.

Exercises

9.1 **Fill in the blanks with *take* or *bring*.**

1. Are you going shopping? ..*Take*.. an umbrella. It's raining.
2. "Don't forget to .... your books to class tomorrow!" the teacher said to the students.
3. Are you going to the kitchen? Can you .... me a glass of milk?
4. .... your camera with you when you go to Bangkok. It's beautiful there.
5. Are you going to the post office? Would you .... these letters and mail them, please?

9.2 **Fill in the blanks with *take* or *bring back*.**

1. Can I .... this book to read tonight? I'll .... it .... tomorrow.
2. When she went to Japan, she .... me .... some delicious green tea.
3. Here, ... my umbrella. You can .... it .... tomorrow.

9.3 **Match the words on the left with the words on the right. Draw lines.**

1. Yesterday he brought me   a. these papers, please.
2. You have to take   b. bring your guitar.
3. Come to our party, and   c. your passport when you travel.
4. Go to the secretary, and take   d. food to the party.
5. Everybody is going to bring   e. some flowers.

9.4 **Fill in the blanks with the correct form of *bring* or *take*.**

1. She always ..*brings*.. me presents. Yesterday she .... me some chocolates.
2. Hi! I've .... you some flowers. I hope you like them!
3. I .... 72 photographs when I was in Rio de Janeiro.
4. She .... my book yesterday, but she's going to .... it back tomorrow.

9.5 **Are you in your English class now? If yes, look at (a). If no, look at (b).**

(a) Name three things you always bring to class.
(b) Name three things you always take to class.

9.6 **Name three things someone has brought you recently.**

Get

A *Get* with adjectives: for changes

It's light. ———⟶ It's **getting** dark. ———⟶ It's dark.

She's sick. ———⟶ She's **getting** better. ———⟶ She's better. / She's well.

I'm **getting** tired. I want to go to bed.　It's raining! I'm **getting** wet!

B *Get* with nouns

If you **don't have** something, you can
get [obtain, find, or receive] it.

I want to send a postcard. I have to **get** a stamp.
I've finished school. Now I want to **get** a job.
I'm going to the store to **get** a newspaper.
Where can I **get** a taxi?

C *Get to* [arrive at / reach] a place

A: How can I **get to** the airport?　B: Take the airport bus at the bus
　station.
A: When you **get to** São Paulo, call me.　B: OK, give me your number.

D Other phrases with *get*

Maria and David are **getting married** in June.
When you **get back** from Hong Kong,
　call me. [return / come home]
When I **get home**, I take off my shoes.
I'll probably **get there** at 6 o'clock, so please call
　me at 6:30. (*not* get ~~to~~ home or get ~~to~~ there.)

Exercises

10.1 Complete these sentences using (a), (b), or (c).

1. I studied too much, and I got (a) hot (b) tired (c) sick.
2. I ate too much, and I got (a) hot (b) tired (c) sick.
3. I sat in the sun too long, and now I'm getting (a) hot (b) tired (c) sick.

10.2 Complete these sentences using *get* and a word from the box.

better	1. The sun is going down. It *'s getting dark* .
light	2. When the sun comes up, it ....
dark	3. He's in the hospital, but he ....
cold	4. It's raining! I ....!
wet	5. Please close the window. I ....

10.3 What do you *get* if . . .

1. you want to mail a letter? *a stamp* ....
2. you want to earn some money? ....
3. you want to write something down? ....
4. you want to read the news? ....
5. you want to go to the airport? ....

10.4 Fill in the blanks using *get.*

Singapore (departs 4:55 pm)   Vancouver (arrives 11:05 am)

1. This plane .... Vancouver at 11:05 am.

    university (25 minutes)   my house

2. The bus from the university .... my house in 25 minutes.

    hotel   airport

3. A: How .... the airport?
   B: Take a taxi. The bus is very slow!

10.5 Answer the questions.

1. In your country, how old are people (usually) when they get married?
2. When do most people get married? Which day? Which month(s)?
3. What time do you get home every day? How do you get there?

UNIT 11 Phrasal verbs

A What are phrasal verbs?

Phrasal verbs have two parts:
a verb (e.g., *get*, *go*) + a particle (e.g., *up*, *on*).

get up/along/over
I **got up** at 6:30 this morning. I'm tired now.
I hated my sister when I was young, but now
  we **get along** very well.
He **got over** his cold quickly. [He got better.]

turn on/off/up/down
He always **turns on** the TV at 9 o'clock to
  watch the news.
It's a sunny day. **Turn off** the light.
Turn up the TV. I can't hear it.
Turn down the TV. It's too loud.

go on/off
What's **going on** here? [What's happening?]
My alarm clock **went off** at 7 a.m.
  [rang; made noise]

come on/up
Come on! [Hurry!] We're late.
What topics **came up** at the meeting? [were discussed]

put on (clothes)
It's cold and windy outside. **Put on** your coat.

B One phrasal verb, different meanings

turn down
She **turned down** the stereo. [made it not so loud]
She **turned down** the invitation. [refused it]

take off

The plane **takes off** at 12:30.
[departs or leaves the ground]

He **took off** his shoes.
[removed them from his feet]

Tip: Write down any phrasal verbs you see or hear on a special page in your notebook.

Exercises

11.1 Match a sentence on the left with a sentence on the right. Draw lines.

1. The alarm clock rang.
2. The evening news is on soon.
3. Her boyfriend left her.
4. I'm trying to work.
5. It's raining today.
6. I don't want to take that job.

a. Then turn it down.
b. Please turn down that music.
c. It's time to get up.
d. Put on your raincoat.
e. She got over it quickly.
f. Turn on the TV.

11.2 Put the correct particles in these sentences.

1. It's dark in here. Turn ...*on*... the lights.
2. Our plane takes .... at 6:25 and lands at 7:50.
3. Come ....! It's time to get ....
4. The children took .... their school uniforms when they got home.
5. It's time to turn .... the TV and go to bed now.
6. That teacher always gets .... with her students.
7. The subject of money always comes .... when he talks to his parents.
8. When they got to the beach, she put .... her swimsuit and ran down to the water.

11.3 What is going on in these pictures? Use one of the phrasal verbs from page 24 to describe each picture.

1. ...*The plane is taking off.*...

3. ....

2. ....

4. ....

11.4 Organize the words on page 24 into groups in any way that makes sense to you; for example, clothes, movement.

11.5 Replace the underlined words with a phrasal verb from the box.

get over	take off	turn up	go on

took off

1. I <u>removed</u> my hat and coat.
2. What's <u>happening</u> here?
3. <u>Make</u> the radio <u>louder</u>. I can't hear it.
4. He <u>got better from</u> the flu quickly.

Everyday things

A   Things you do every day

| I wake up | get up | go to the bathroom | have breakfast |

listen to the radio   go to work   come home   make dinner

call (*or* phone) a friend   watch TV   take a bath   go to sleep

B   Sometimes I . . .

do the laundry   clean the house   go for a walk   write letters

C   Questions about everyday things

How often do you read the newspaper / watch TV?
   Three times a week. / Every day.
What time do you get up / go to work?
   Seven o'clock. / Half past eight.
How do you go to work?
   By bus/train/car.   *or*   On foot.

D   Usually/normally (what I do typically)

You can say **I usually/normally** get up at 8 o'clock, *but* today I got up at 8:30.
(*not* I ~~used to~~ get up / ~~I'm used to~~ get up at 8 o'clock.)

Exercises

12.1 Complete the sentences about *yourself*.

1. I usually wake up at .... on weekdays.
2. I usually have .... for breakfast.
3. I normally go to work by/on ....
4. I usually have a cup of coffee/tea at .... o'clock.
5. I usually .... a bath/shower at about .... a.m./p.m.

12.2 What do they usually do?

1. He *listens to the radio every morning* .
   (every morning)

2. He d.........................
   ....
   ....
   (every Saturday)

3. She c.........................
   ....
   ....
   (every weekend)

4. He w.........................
   ....
   ....
   (every evening)

5. She g.........................
   ....
   ....
   (every Sunday)

12.3 Ask questions.

Topic	Question	Answer
1. get up	What **time do you get up?**	Seven-thirty, usually.
2. go for a walk	How . . . ?	Every Saturday.
3. go to work	How . . . ?	By train.
4. have dinner	When . . . ?	Usually between 6 and 7 o'clock.

Talking

A   *Say*

Use **say** when you report someone's words.
    She **said,** "This is terrible!"
He **said that** he wanted some coffee.

Use **say** when you ask about language.
    A: **How do you say** "book" in Spanish?   B: "Libro."

We **say hello / good-bye,**   **please / thank you,**
happy birthday / Happy New Year / Congratulations.

B   *Tell*

Tell can be followed immediately by a person (e.g., **tell** me, him, her, etc.).
Say is not followed immediately by a person.
    He **told me** his name. (*not* He ~~said me~~ his name.)

Use **tell** when you want to know how to get to a place.
    Can you tell me where the bus station is, please? (*not* Can you ~~say me~~ . . . ?)

Use **tell** with other **wh**-words too (**when, how, why, where**); e.g., you can **tell**
someone how to do something, **where** something is, **why** something happened.
    He **told me how** to send a fax. **Tell me when** you want to go home.

You can **tell someone the time / a story / a joke / your name / address /**
telephone number.

C   *Ask*

Ask is used for questions.
    My sister **asked me** where I was going. *or* My sister asked (me),
        "Where are you going?"

You can **ask someone the time / a question.**
Ask someone to do something, and **ask someone for something.**
    I **asked him to** turn off his radio.
        (*or* I said, "Please turn off your radio.")
    She **asked** the waiter **for** the bill.
        (*or* She said, "Can I have the bill, please?")

D   *Speak/talk/answer/reply*

Note the different uses of these verbs:
    Do you **speak** Korean? (*not* Do you ~~talk~~ Korean?)
        I like **talking to** you.
    I'll **answer** the telephone / the door. [pick up the phone
        when it rings / open the door to see who is there]
    I wrote him a letter, but he didn't **reply.**   *or*
        He didn't **reply to** my letter. [He did not send me a
        letter back.] (for letters, faxes, e-mails, etc.)

Exercises

13.1   **Fill in the blanks with the correct form of *say* or *tell*.**

1. "Come here!" the police officer ..*said*...
2. She .... me her name.
3. I .... good-bye to him.
4. "Please .... me a story," the little boy ....
5. Can you .... me where the Park Hotel is, please?
6. The teacher .... that the students were very good.

13.2   **What do you say?**

1. You want to know where the subway station is.
   Can ..*you tell me where*...... ..*the subway station is*.... ?

2. You want to know the word for "tea" in Chinese.
   How ....?

3. You want to know the time.
   Excuse me, can you ....
   ....?

4. You want to know when the exam is.
   Can you ....?

5. The telephone rings. You are in the bathroom.
   (*To your friend*) Can you ....
   ....?

13.3   **Circle the correct verb to complete the phrases.**

1. Ask / (Tell) / Say   someone a joke
2. Reply / Reply to / Answer   the door
3. Answer / Ask for / Ask   the check
4. Reply to / Reply / Ask   a letter
5. Tell / Say / Speak   happy birthday
6. Talk / Reply / Talk to   a friend
7. Ask / Say / Talk   someone to help you

13.4   **On the left are some words in different languages. Can you match them with the sentences on the right? Draw lines.**

1. La cuenta, por favor.   a. Say Happy New Year in Portuguese.
2. Berapa ini?   b. Say good afternoon in Japanese.
3. Feliz Ano Novo   c. Ask for the bill in Spanish.
4. Kon nichi wa.   d. Ask how much something costs in Malay.

UNIT 14   Movement

A   Without transportation

walk   swim   climb   run   dance   fall   jump   jog

B   Transportation

You **go by** car/plane/bus/train/bike/motorcycle/ship/taxi/subway.
(*not* by ~~a~~ car)

You **take** a bus/train/taxi/plane,
and you **take** the subway.

You **ride** a bicycle/train /
motorcycle/horse.

You **drive** a car/bus/taxi/truck.

The pilot **flies** a plane.

How did you get to Mexico City?
   We **flew** there.

If you **catch** the bus, train, or plane, you arrive in time to get it.
If you **miss** the bus, train, or plane, you arrive too late to get it.

You **arrive in** or **at** a place (*not* ~~to~~ a place).
   The train arrived in Tokyo on time.
   The plane arrived at Kennedy Airport two hours late.

Tip: When you are traveling, you will probably see a lot of signs and notices
in English. Make a note of any new words and expressions you see.

(See Unit 41 [Travel] for more words about transportation.)

C   Moving objects

Please pass the salt.

Can I help you carry
your luggage?

14.1 Fill in the blanks with verbs from A on page 30. Use the correct form.

1. Jack likes to ...*jog*... around the park every morning.
2. Everyone .... at the party last night.
3. Every morning Alicia .... ten laps in the swimming pool before breakfast.
4. Ana can .... very fast. She has won a lot of races.
5. Roberto likes to .... mountains.
6. The old lady .... on her way home and broke her hip.
7. Aki .... into the swimming pool and quickly .... to the other side.
8. It is much better for you to .... to work than to go by car.

14.2 *Ride, drive, fly, go by,* or *take*?
Write the correct word(s).

1. Do you know how to ...*drive*... a car?
2. He works for an airline. He .... a plane.
3. I usually .... a taxi when it rains.
4. She goes away from home a lot. She .... a truck.
5. I prefer to .... a bus than .... car.
6. Would you like to .... an elephant?

14.3 Answer these questions. Use answers like *every day, twice a week, once a year,* or *never*.

1. How often do you walk to work or school? ..*I walk to work every day*.....
2. Do you have a bicycle? How often do you ride it?
3. How often do you go swimming? Do you swim in the ocean or in a swimming pool?
4. How often do you go jogging?
5. How often do you drive a car?
6. How often do you go dancing?

14.4 What things do we ask people to pass at the dinner table? Write down *Please pass* + a noun six times.

Please pass the sugar.

14.5 Put these sentences in the past tense with the word *yesterday*.

1. Bill runs a mile every day. ..*Bill ran a mile yesterday*...
2. Mei-Li often drives her grandmother to the mall.
3. Maria catches the 8:45 train to the city every day.
4. I sometimes take a taxi home from the train station.
5. Tom often falls when he rides his bike.

Conjunctions and connecting words

A Conjunctions

Conjunctions join two parts of a sentence and help to show the connection between the two parts of the sentence. Note the use of commas before some conjunctions.

Conjunction	Function	Example
and	tells you more	We got home and went right to bed.
but	makes a contrast	They are rich, but they aren't happy.
because	answers the question *why?*	We went home because we were tired.
so	tells you the result	We went home early, so we missed the end of the concert.
when	answers the questions *when* or *at what time?*	We went home when it started to rain.
before, after	answers the question *what happened first?*	We went home before the concert ended. We went home after the singer sang his first song.
although/though	tells you something is surprising	We went home although/though we did not really want to.
if	makes a condition	We will go home if we are tired.

B Other connecting words

The words in this chart make connections between words and phrases.

Word	Function	Example
only	says something is smaller or less than usual	He sleeps only three hours every night.
even	says something is surprising or unusual	Everyone was on time for the meeting, even Pat, who's usually late.
like	makes a comparison	She looks like her dad.
than	used after a comparative adjective or adverb	Ann is older than Chris. / She works harder than he does.
also / too / as well	says something is in addition	He works in the store, and she does also / too / as well.

Exercises

15.1 Choose one of the <u>underlined</u> words to complete the sentence.

1. Sam liked school (because)/although/if he had many friends there.
2. Sam graduated from school, so/but/and he got a job driving a truck.
3. He hadn't traveled much but/before/after he became a truck driver.
4. Sam got carsick a lot, when/if/so he quit his job.
5. He got a job as a cook at a cafe because/although/and he had no qualifications.
6. He will stay at the cafe when/if/though he likes it there.

15.2 Write down ten sentences from the chart below.
Use each conjunction once.

	after	she loves him.
	although	she doesn't love him.
Mary agreed to marry Paul	and	she loved him.
	because	she didn't love him.
	before	they had two sons.
	but	he moves to Hollywood.
	if	he moved to Hollywood.
Mary will marry Paul	so	he was a rock star.
	though	they decided to go into business
	when	together.

15.3 Write each conjunction in A on page 32 in your own language.

15.4 Fill in the blanks with words from the chart in B on page 32.

I love swimming, and my brother loves swimming (1) .... Almost everyone in my family loves swimming. (2) .... my grandmother swims every day. She swims (3) .... a fish. (4) .... my father doesn't like it very much. I can swim better (5) .... my father.

15.5 Think about your family and your habits. Write sentences about your habits with *only, even, than, like, also, too,* and *as well.*

I play tennis and my mother plays too. My mother plays better than I do.

15.6 Complete these sentences about *yourself.*

1. I am learning English because ....
2. I'll learn more English if ....
3. I am learning English, and ....
4. I am learning English although ....
5. I started learning English when ....
6. I can speak some English, so ....

Time words (1): days, months, and seasons

A   **Basic time words**

There are:

365 days in a year.	24 hours in a day.
12 months in a year.	60 minutes in an hour. (*Note:* **an** hour)
52 weeks in a year.	60 seconds in a minute.
7 days in a week.	100 years in a century.

B   **Days of the week**

Sunday, Monday, Tuesday, Wednesday, Thursday, Friday, Saturday

The names of the days always begin with a capital letter in English.

Saturday + Sunday = the **weekend** (in most English-speaking countries)

the day before
yesterday   ←   yesterday   ←   today   →   tomorrow   →   the day after
tomorrow

Monday **morning** = Monday (before 12 noon)
Monday **afternoon** = Monday (between 12 noon and about 5 or 6 p.m.)
Monday **evening** = Monday (from about 5 or 6 p.m. until 9 or 10 p.m.)

We say **on** + days of the week: on Monday, on Saturday, etc.
   I saw her **on Friday / on Tuesday** evening.

We say **on/over** + the weekend.
   I went skiing **on the weekend / over the weekend.**

C   **Months and seasons**

Months: January, February, March, April, May, June, July, August, September,
   October, November, December

The names of the months always begin with a capital letter in English.

Some countries have four seasons: spring, summer, fall/autumn, and winter.

spring   summer   fall/autumn   winter

We say **in** + months/seasons: in July, in May, in (the) fall, in (the) summer, etc.
   My birthday is **in March.** (*not* ~~on~~ March) Birds sing **in (the) spring.**

Tip: Write the day and date in English whenever you do an English exercise.

Exercises

16.1 Complete the sentences with a word from A on page 34.

1. There are 3,600 seconds in ..*an hour*.....
2. There are 1,200 months in ....
3. There are 168 hours in ....
4. There are 8,760 hours in ....

16.2 Say (a) the days of the week and (b) the months of the year.

16.3 Complete this poem about the number of days in each month.

Thirty days has S*eptember*....,
A................., J..................., and N.................... .
All the rest have ....,
Except for F.................. alone:
Which has but twenty-eight, in fine,
Till **leap year** gives it .... [every four years]

16.4 These abbreviations are often used for the days of the week and the months. Write out the names in full.

1. Mon.   4. Sat.   7. Apr.   10. Sept.
2. Aug.   5. Wed.   8. Thurs.   11. Tues.
3. Oct.   6. Jan.   9. Feb.   12. Nov.

16.5 What are the next few letters in each case? Explain why.

1. S   M   T   W   ?   ?   ?
2. J   F   M   A   M   J   J   ?   ?   ?   ?   ?

16.6 Correct the five mistakes in this paragraph.

I'm going to a party on saturday for Jill's birthday. Her birthday is on tuesday, but she wanted to have the party on the Weekend. She's having a barbecue. I think spring is a good time to have a party because of the weather. I love going to barbecues on the spring. My birthday is in Winter, and it's too cold to eat outside!

16.7 Quiz: How quickly can you answer these questions?

1. How many seconds are there in a quarter of an hour?
2. What day is it today?
3. What day will it be the day after tomorrow?
4. What day was it the day before yesterday?
5. What is the seventh month?
6. What month is it?
7. What century is it?
8. How many minutes are there in half an hour?
9. What month is your birthday in?
10. What day was it yesterday?

UNIT 17 Time words (2)

A Time in relation to now

Now means at this moment. **Then** means at another moment (in the past or in the future).

It is 10 **o'clock** now.
I got up 2 **hours ago, at** 8 o'clock.
I'll eat lunch in 2 hours.
Then it will be 12 o'clock.

for two years [for + a period of time]
from 1997 to 1999   *1997 → 1999*
from 2017 to 2019

I lived in Brazil **for two years.** I worked in Rio **from 1997 to 1999.**

last year / last week / last Saturday
next year / next week / next summer

It is July now.
Last month it was June.
Next month it will be August.

When we talk about time in general, we talk about **the past, the present,** and **the future.**

> **In the past** people didn't have computers.
> People may travel to Mars **in the future.**
> I'll be with you **in a moment.** [a very short time]
> Jane is on the phone **at the moment.** [now]
> See you **soon!** [in a short time] We met **recently.** [not long ago]

B Frequency adverbs

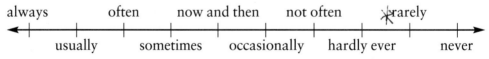

always   often   now and then   not often   rarely
        usually   sometimes   occasionally   hardly ever   never

It **always** snows in Canada during the winter.
It **often** rains in Seattle.
The temperature in London **hardly ever** gets to 35°C. [almost never]
It **never** snows in Singapore.

Note the use of **a** in these expressions of frequency:
> once [one time] a week: I go swimming **once a week,** every Saturday.
> twice [two times] a day: I brush my teeth **twice a day.**
> three times a month: I play soccer **three or four times a month.**
> four times a year: I see my uncle **four times a year.**

Exercises

17.1 **Fill in the blanks with prepositions from A on page 36.**

(1) ......*In*...... the past, Rosa worked in many different countries. She worked in Hong Kong (2) .... three years, (3) .... 1996 (4) .... 1999. (5) .... the moment Rosa is working in Tokyo. She will stay there (6) .... two more years.

17.2 **Read the sentences and answer the questions.**

1. Peter will get his exam results very soon. Do you think Peter will get them next year, next month, or tomorrow?
2. Sue and Bill met for the first time recently. Do you think they first met last year, six months ago, or a week ago?
3. I'll help you in a moment. Do you think I'll help you next week, in two hours, or in a few minutes?

17.3 **Are these sentences true about *you*? If not, write them out correctly. Use other frequency adverbs from B on page 36.**

1. I always go swimming on Fridays.   *I sometimes go swimming on Fridays.*
   I often go swimming on Saturdays.
2. I usually go to school/work by bus.
3. I hardly ever play soccer.
4. I occasionally watch TV.
5. I rarely drink milk.
6. I often wear a hat.
7. I rarely eat chocolate.
8. I always go to bed at 10.
9. I never go to the theater.

17.4 **Look at the table and make sentences using expressions like *once a week*, *three times a month*, etc.**

	Play tennis	*Practice the piano*	*Have a business meeting in Toronto*
John	Mondays and Thursdays	Saturdays	the first Friday of every month
Sally and Amy	Tuesdays, Fridays, and Saturdays	every morning and every evening	once in January, March, May, July, August, and December every year

17.5 **Write a paragraph about your own life using as many as possible of the words and expressions from page 36.**

I usually get up early. I always have a cup of coffee . . .

UNIT
18 Places

A General place words

Come **here,** please. [to me, to where I am]
Have you ever been to Peru? I'm going **there** in May. [to another place, not
    here]
I'm coming **back** from Vietnam in April. [returning here, to this place again]
There are books and papers **everywhere** in my room. [in all parts / all places]
(See Unit 7.)

B Positions

the **top** of the mountain   the **middle** of the road   the **bottom** of the glass

the **front** of the car   the **side** of the car   the **back** of the car

the **beginning** of
the book

the **end** of the book

C *Left* and *right*

his **left** hand

his **right** hand

On Main Street, there is a pharmacy **on the left** and a restaurant **on the right.**

D *Home* and *away*

Is Mary **home / at home?** [in her house/apartment]
    No, she's **out.** [shopping / at work / at school]
    No, she's **away.** [in another town/city or country]
    No, she's **out of town.** [in another town or city]
    Mary is going **abroad** next year. [to another country]

38

Exercises

18.1   Fill in the blanks with *here* or *there*.

1. Are you coming .... next week? (See Unit 7 for **Come.**)
2. This letter is for a teacher at the university. Can you take it ....?
   (See Unit 8 for **Take.**)
3. Please bring it .... (See Unit 9 for **Bring.**)
4. I want to leave this letter in Ms. Ito's office. Are you going ....?

18.2   Complete the sentences.

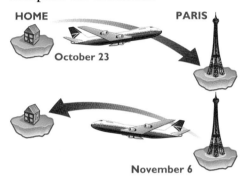

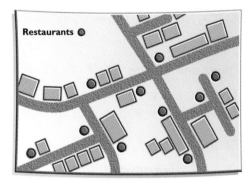

1. What is Mary doing on
   November 6th?
   She's coming ....

2. Are there any restaurants in
   Oakland?
   Yes, there are restaurants ....

18.3   Mark the positions on the tree and on the bus.

1. the top of the tree
2. the bottom of the tree
3. the front of the bus
4. the side of the bus
5. the back of the bus

18.4   Answer the questions about *yourself* and about this book.

1. Are you studying English at home or abroad?
2. Are you going away this year?
3. What do you have in your left or right hand at the moment?
4. Where is the unit on **Have** in this book? (beginning/middle/end?)
5. Where is the unit on **Feelings**? (beginning/middle/end?)

18.5   Fill in the blanks with *out, away, out of town,* or *abroad.*

1. I'd like to work .... and learn about a new country.
2. Is Luis here? No, he's ...., but he'll be back in a minute.
3. I'm going .... tomorrow, to my sister's. She lives about 100 miles
   north of here.
4. When we go ...., we like to go .... and see new countries.

Manner

Manner = **how** we do something or **the way** we do something.

A *Fast* and *slow*

This car goes very **fast**. It's a **fast** car.   This car goes very **slowly**. It's a **slow** car.

B *Right* and *wrong*

This sentence is **right**. [correct]   I like coffee very much.   ✓
This sentence is **wrong**. [not correct]   I like very much coffee.   ✗

C *Loud* and *quiet*

The music is too **loud**.   It's very **quiet** here.

The teacher speaks very **quietly**. We can't hear him.
She sang **loudly**. [Her voice was loud.]

D *Well* and *badly*

She's a **good** swimmer. She swims **well**.   He's a **bad** swimmer. He swims **badly**.

E *Way*

Way means **how** someone does something.

He's speaking **in a friendly way**.   She's speaking **in an unfriendly way**.

Exercises

19.1 **Complete the sentences.**

1. This train is **slow**. It goes very ..*slowly*........ .
2. She is a **bad** driver. She drives very ....
3. He is always **loud**. He speaks very ....
4. He's a **fast** swimmer. He swims very ....
5. That little girl is **quiet**. She speaks ....
6. He's a **good** English speaker. He speaks English ....

19.2 **Which do you think is better? Use your dictionary if you want to.**

1. A loud person or a quiet person?
2. A fast bus or a slow bus?
3. A friendly person or an unfriendly person?
4. A right answer or a wrong answer?
5. To speak politely or impolitely?
6. To speak in a strange way or in a normal way?

19.3 **Find six words from page 40.**

```
w  r  o  n  g  b
e  c  i  g  l  a
l  u  b  b  a  d
l  o  u  d  h  l
s  f  a  s  t  y
```

19.4 **Use a dictionary. Are the definitions right or wrong?**

Word	Definition	Right (✔) Wrong (✘)
suddenly	very slowly	✘
sadly	in an unhappy way	
strangely	not in a normal way	
quickly	very slowly	
easily	with no difficulty	

19.5 **Write at least five sentences about yourself and your friends/family. Use the new words from page 40.**

My sister plays tennis well. I sing badly.

Irregular verbs

Most English verbs are regular, but some common verbs in English are irregular. The forms here are the base form (**have, go, get**), the past tense (**had, went, got**), and the past participle (**had, gone, gotten**). When you learn a new irregular verb, add it to one of the groups of verbs on this page.

A **All forms the same**

cost	cost	cost	cut	cut	cut	hurt	hurt	hurt
let	let	let	put	put	put	shut	shut	shut

B **Two different forms**

beat	beat	beaten	lose	lost	lost	shoot	shot	shot
find	found	found	make	made	made	sit	sat	sat
have	had	had	pay	paid	paid**	stand	stood	stood
hear	heard	heard	say	said	said***	understand	understood	understood
become	became	become	come	came	come	run	ran	run
bend	bent	bent	send	sent	sent	spend	spent	spent
dig	dug	dug	win	won	won			
feel	felt	felt	leave	left	left	read	read	read*
keep	kept	kept	meet	met	met	sleep	slept	slept
bring	brought	brought	catch	caught	caught	teach	taught	taught
buy	bought	bought	fight	fought	fought	think	thought	thought
sell	sold	sold	tell	told	told			

34

C **Three different forms**

be	was/were	been	fall	fell	fallen	see	saw	seen
do	did	done	give	gave	given			
eat	ate	eaten	go	went	gone	take	took	taken
begin	began	begun	ring	rang	rung	sink	sank	sunk
drink	drank	drunk	sing	sang	sung	swim	swam	swum
break	broke	broken	speak	spoke	spoken	wake	woke	woken
choose	chose	chosen	steal	stole	stolen			
drive	drove	driven	ride	rode	ridden	write	wrote	written
fly	flew	flown	know	knew	known	throw	threw	thrown
get	got	gotten	forget	forgot	forgotten			
tear	tore	torn	wear	wore	worn			

29

*The three forms of **read** are all spelled the same but not pronounced the same.
Pay/paid/paid are irregular in spelling but not in pronunciation.
***The vowel in **said** is pronounced differently from the vowel in **paid**.

(See pages 126–127 for a list of irregular verbs.)

Exercises

20.1   Do you know what the verbs on page 42 mean? Write the meaning of each verb in your own language. Use a dictionary if you want to.

20.2   Write these words out in their three forms. Use a dictionary. Then find a verb on page 42 with the opposite meaning. Write its three forms.

1. open   *open, opened, opened; opposite – shut, shut, shut*
2. give   5. sit   8. rise
3. come   6. arrive   9. win
4. throw   7. remember   10. buy

20.3   Use the pictures to complete this story about Jane's day.

Yesterday Jane (1) ..*woke/got*.. up at 7:00. She (2) .... an apple and (3) .... a cup of tea. She (4) .... a newspaper, and then she got in her car and (5) .... to work. At work she (6) .... some letters. At lunchtime she (7) .... in the park for half an hour, and then she (8) .... a sandwich. After lunch she (9) .... at her desk again and (10) .... some telephone calls. In the evening she (11) .... the office at 6:00 and (12) .... some Japanese visitors. They (13) .... to a restaurant together. After a busy day, Jane (14) .... very well.

1.   2.   3.   4.   5.   6.   7.

8.   9.   10.   11.   12.   13.   14.

20.4   Choose verbs from page 42. Complete the sentences with the correct past participle form.

1. We have ..*swum*........ in the swimming pool every day this week.
2. We haven't .... to Europe in years.
3. Have you .... lunch yet?
4. I have .... a lot of time doing homework this semester.
5. I've .... Celia for years. She's my best friend.
6. A: Have you .... the latest *Star Wars* movie?
   B: Yes, ten times!

UNIT
21 Common uncountable words

A What is countable and uncountable?

apples

shoes

plates

COUNTABLE (You can count them and make them plural: four apples, two shoes)

sugar

money

luggage

UNCOUNTABLE (You can't count it and can't make it plural: *not* three ~~luggages~~)

Can I have **three apples** and **some sugar**, please?
Are these **shoes** yours? Is this **luggage** yours?

B Everyday uncountable words

This **furniture** is expensive.

The **traffic** is heavy today.

There is some bad **news** today.

I'll give you some **advice** about your future.

They can give you some useful **information** about Taiwan.

The **weather** is terrible today.

I need some fresh **air**.

This is hard **work**.

Air **travel** is faster than train **travel**.

C Food

A lot of uncountable nouns are kinds of food and drink.

rice   spaghetti   butter   bread   beef   milk   water

Note: When you say how much, use containers (or units) that you can count (e.g., three cups of rice, two quarts of milk, a pound of butter).

Tip: When you learn a new noun, write it down in a phrase that shows if it is countable or uncountable.

44

Exercises

21.1 Fill in the blanks with an uncountable noun from page 44.

1. I'd like to buy a car, but I don't have enough ..*money*........ .
2. Cows give us .... and ....
3. If you don't know what to do, ask your parents or teacher for some
   ....
4. There is always a lot of .... in the center of the city.
5. Somsak graduates from college next month and is already looking for
   ....

21.2 Match the words. There may be more than one answer.

1. heavy   information
2. useful   travel
3. bad   water
4. modern   traffic
5. fried   news
6. cold   furniture
7. space   rice

21.3 Find an adjective to go with the uncountable nouns in the box.

cold weather, Canadian money

weather	money	sugar	traffic	advice	air
work	spaghetti	butter	milk	tea	coffee

21.4 Fill in the blanks with the correct form of the verb *be*.

1. Work ..*is/was*....... the most important thing in Sam's life.
2. Their furniture .... very old and very beautiful.
3. Those chairs .... very expensive.
4. The weather in Japan .... best in the fall.
5. The news .... better today than it .... yesterday.
6. How many apples .... there in a pound?
7. Spaghetti with tomato sauce .... very good.

21.5 Correct the mistakes.

1. The news ~~are~~ not very good today.
   The news is not very good today.
2. I'd like some informations about your country.
3. Let me give you an advice.
4. Cook these rice for thirty minutes.
5. Mary is looking for a new work.
6. There's usually a better weather in the east then in the west.
7. We should buy some new furnitures.
8. We went on two long travels last year.

Common adjectives: good and bad things

A (+) "good" adjectives

a **good** restaurant   a **better** restaurant   the **best** restaurant in town
3 stars ★★★   4 stars ★★★★   5 stars ★★★★★
This restaurant is **better than** that one.

nice/beautiful/great/wonderful/excellent

A: That's a **nice** jacket.   A: It's a **beautiful** day today!
B: Thank you.   B: Yes, it is.

A: Do you want to go to the beach on Sunday?   Mary's a **wonderful** person.
B: That's a **great** idea / an **excellent** idea!   Everybody likes her.
    [very, very good]

When you answer and want to say how you feel:
    A: The train arrives at 6 o'clock; dinner is at 7:30.
    B: **Great!/Wonderful!/Terrific!/Perfect!**

B (−) "bad" adjectives

bad (**worse** / **the worst**) / **awful** / **disgusting** / **terrible**

bad weather   My hair looks **awful!**

The weather last year was **worse than** this year.
Jane is an **awful** person. No one likes her.
That's an **awful** thing to say.
I had a **terrible** day at work today.
The traffic is **terrible** at 5 o'clock on Fridays.

Note the use of **how**:
    A: I have to get up at 5:30 a.m. tomorrow.
    B: Oh, **how awful!** (*not* how bad)

    A: This bathroom hasn't been cleaned in weeks.
    B: Oh, **how disgusting!**

Exercises

22.1 Fill in the blanks, as in the example.

1. My hair looks .. *awful/terrible* .... I have to go to the hairdresser.
2. The weather's .... today. Let's go to the park.
3. The traffic is .... in the city. Take the train.
4. That's a(n) .... idea! Let's do it!
5. How ....! Three exams on the same day!
6. What a .... house! The beach is only 300 feet away!

22.2 What can you say when someone says to you . . .?

1. Do you like my new jacket?   *Yes, it's very nice.*   or   *Yes, it's beautiful.*
2. I have to get up at 4:30 tomorrow morning.
3. Let's go out for dinner tonight.
4. (*In your town*) Excuse me. Is there a good restaurant in this town?
5. What kind of person is your English teacher?
6. There's a bug in your soup!

22.3 Match a description on the left with an expression on the right.

1. Blue sky, sunny, 72°F   a. Wonderful news
2. 5 stars (★★★★★), very famous   b. Awful weather
3. Bad person. Nobody likes him/her   c. Nice weather
4. 95 out of 100 in an exam   d. An excellent idea
5. Dark skies, wind, rain   e. The best hotel in town
6. We can take a taxi   f. An awful person

22.4 Use a dictionary. Put these new words into the *good* or *bad* column.

dreadful   fabulous   fine   gorgeous   horrendous   horrible   superb

good (+)	bad (−)
	dreadful

22.5 Look at the adjectives in 22.4. Think of two nouns to go with each adjective.

dreadful news / a dreadful movie

UNIT 23 Common adjectives: people

A Saying positive (+) / good things about people

Nice is the most common word used for people who we like / who are good.
> Mary's very **nice**.
> Richard's a **nice** man.

If you want to make **nice** stronger, you can use **wonderful**.
> Ron is a **wonderful** teacher. All the students love him.
> But we don't say "Mary is ~~very~~ wonderful." Just say "Mary is wonderful."

If someone is good to other people, you can use **kind**.
> She's very **kind**; she helps me with the children.

Other "good" things about people
> My friend Antonio is very **easygoing**. [relaxed, easy to be with]
> Marta's a **happy** person. [≠ **an unhappy** person]
> All my friends are more **intelligent** than I am. [smart, good at school subjects]

John is very **thoughtful**. [kind, thinks about the feelings of others]
He always brings his mother flowers.

That little boy is very **well behaved**. [good, behaves well]

B Saying negative (−) / bad things about people

Laura is **not very nice**.
Nancy is an **awful** woman; nobody likes her.
Al can be **nasty** when he's in a bad mood. [says unkind, offensive things]
My aunt is a **difficult** person. [not easy to please] She is never happy.
That waiter is **stupid**. I asked for coffee and he brought me tea! When I asked for coffee again, he brought me milk! (**Stupid** is a very strong word.)
I don't like **selfish** people. [people who think only of themselves]
Sometimes my teenage son can be **childish**. [behaves like a child]

C Prepositions

Jean was very nice/kind **to** me when I was in the hospital.
You were nasty **to** me yesterday!
It was nice/kind/thoughtful **of** you to remember my birthday.

Exercises

23.1 **What do you think B said? Complete the sentences.**

Let me carry your bag.

1. A: Mary's very nice.
   B: She's more than nice, she's .... !
2. A: George wasn't very nice to you, was he?
   B: He was really .... !
3. A: Let me carry your bag.
   B: Thanks, that's ....
4. A: Is your little brother a good boy?
   B: Yes, he's very ....

23.2 **Complete the word puzzle. Use the letters of *thoughtful* and other words from page 48.**

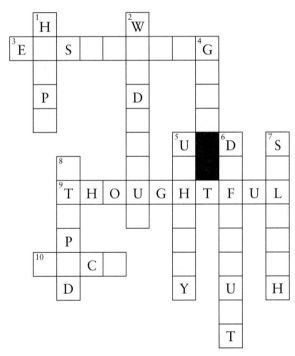

23.3 **Circle the words that describe *you*.**

I am . . . easygoing.   sometimes difficult.   kind to animals.

sometimes stupid.   nice to my friends.   nasty to some people.

selfish.   intelligent.   sometimes childish.

23.4 **Fill in the correct prepositions.**

1. The teacher is never nasty ..*to*.... the students.
2. It is nice .... you to help me.
3. Pat was very kind .... me when I needed a friend.
4. It was nice .... him to call me.

Words and prepositions

A Verb + preposition

I **listen to** the radio in bed every morning.
I'll be a few minutes late. Can you **wait for** me?
I **asked for** coffee, not tea.
Where do I **pay for** this magazine?
This book **belongs to** Sarah Smith.

What are you **thinking about**?
Helena **thanked** her father **for** the present.
Jack **apologized for** being late.

B Same verb, different preposition

Some verbs have different meanings when they are
used with different prepositions (e.g., **look**).

I love **looking at** old photographs.
If you want to find something,
 (e.g., your key), you have to **look for** it.
Look up the word in the dictionary if you
 don't know what it means. [try to find
 information, usually in a reference book]
You **look forward to** something good in the future (e.g., a trip or a party).

C Adjective + preposition

I'm **good at** science but **bad at** math.
I'm **interested in** (hearing) all your news.
He is **afraid of** mice.
John is **proud of** winning a medal, and his mother is **proud of** him, too.

D *Be used to / Get used to*

You **are used to** what you know well or always do. [**accustomed to**]
I'm used to the traffic downtown.
I'm used to getting up early. (*not* I'm used to ~~get~~ up)
You have to **get used to** something new.
I'm getting used to my new schedule.
I'm getting used to driving on the left side of the road. (*not* getting used to ~~drive~~)

Note: Prepositions are followed by a noun (Jo is **good at tennis**) *or* the **-ing**
form of the verb (Jo is **good at playing** the piano) (*not* good at ~~play~~ the piano).

> *Tip:* When you read in English, write down phrases that use prepositions in a
> new way.

Exercises

24.1 Match the phrases to make sentences.

1. John is waiting
2. This umbrella belongs
3. Bill is thinking
4. She apologized
5. Let me pay
6. The children thanked their grandmother

a. about the holidays.
b. for the money.
c. for a bus.
d. for our tickets.
e. to the hotel.
f. for her mistake.

24.2 Complete these sentences with a preposition (*at, to,* etc.) and a noun or pronoun (*me, them, one,* etc.).

1. Ana can't read yet, but she likes looking ..*at books*....
2. I can't find my glasses. Could you help me look ....?
3. Why are you looking .... like that? Is my face dirty?
4. I don't like my job very much. I'm looking ....
5. Alex is going to Hawaii for his vacation. He is looking ....
6. Use your dictionary to look .... if you don't know its meaning.

24.3 Fill in the blanks with a preposition.

Marta is getting used (1) .... her new job and is doing well there. She is very good (2) .... talking to customers. She always listens (3) .... them. She is very interested (4) .... sports, and she belongs (5) .... a tennis club and a swimming club. Her parents were very proud (6) .... her when she won a medal for swimming last year.

24.4 Hiroshi is a visitor to the U.S. from Japan. Make sentences about what he did and did not find strange at first in the U.S.

1. driving on the right ✗ *Hiroshi wasn't used to driving on the right.*
2. traffic jams ✓ *He was used to traffic jams.*
3. eating American food ✗ ....
4. speaking English every day ✗ ....
5. expensive stores ✓ ....
6. American money ✗ ....

24.5 Answer these questions about *yourself*.

1. What were you good at in school? What were you bad at?
2. What do you usually ask for when you go to a cafe?
3. What are you proud of?
4. What are you afraid of?
5. What kind of music do you like listening to?
6. What are you looking forward to?
7. Do you belong to any clubs?
8. Are you used to eating different kinds of food?

Prefixes

Prefixes come at the beginning of words. They can help you to understand what a new word means. Here are some common prefixes.

Prefix	Meaning	Examples
ex	was, but not now	ex-wife, ex-boss
in, im	not	informal, impossible
mis	wrong or badly	misunderstand, misbehave
non	not	nonsmoking, nonresident
pre	before	preschool
re	again	redo, rewrite
un	not	unhappy, unsafe

An **ex-wife** is a wife who is now
    divorced from her husband.
She is my **ex-boss** from my last job.
Informal clothes are clothes like
    jeans and a T-shirt. Formal
    clothes are things like a suit.

informal   formal

If something is **impossible**, you can't do it.
    It is impossible to read with your eyes closed.
If you **misunderstand** something (or someone), you think you understand or
    know it, but you really don't.
If someone **misbehaves**, then he or she is behaving badly.
A **nonsmoking** room is a room where people may not smoke.
A **preschool** is a school for children who are too young
    to go to regular school.
To **redo** something is to do it a
    second time, and to **rewrite**
    something is to write it a
    second time.
Unhappy means sad, the opposite
    of happy.
Unsafe means dangerous, the
    opposite of safe.

Tip: Sometimes words with prefixes have a hyphen (-) (e.g., ex-wife), and
sometimes they don't (e.g., impossible). Use a dictionary when you are not
sure if there is a hyphen.

Exercises

25.1 Complete the sentences with words from the prefix chart on page 52.

1. This part of the restaurant is ..*nonsmoking*..... You can't smoke here.
2. I can't read this. Please .... your homework.
3. In .... English we often say "Hi."
4. I liked school, but my sister was very .... there.
5. Those children cause a lot of trouble. They .... all the time.
6. Don't walk on that sidewalk – the sign says it is ....

25.2 Write your own sentences to show what these words mean.

> ex-wife   ex-boss   redo   impossible   preschool

25.3 What do you think these words and phrases mean? Look at the chart on page 52 to help you.

1. an ex-husband *a husband who is now divorced from his wife*
2. pre-exam nerves
3. an incorrect answer
4. an unread book
5. to retell a story
6. a misspelled word
7. an unfinished letter
8. a nonalcoholic drink
9. to reread a book
10. to rewind a tape

25.4 Find one new example of a word for each prefix from the chart on page 52. Then write a phrase or sentence using your word. Use a dictionary to help you.

ex: *My ex-boyfriend lives near me.*
in: *an incomplete answer*

25.5 Write a paragraph with at least eight of the example words from the chart on page 52.

25.6 Find the negative forms of these words. Use a dictionary if necessary.

1. possible   *impossible*.......
2. comfortable   ....
3. friendly   ....
4. convenient   ....
5. violent   ....
6. sure   ....
7. polite   ....
8. correct   ....

Suffixes

Suffixes come at the end of words. They can help you understand the meaning of a new word. Here are some common suffixes.

Suffix	Meaning	Examples
er, or (noun)	person	worker, swimmer, instructor
er, or (noun)	machine, thing	photocopier, word processor
ful (adjective)	full of	useful, beautiful
ology (noun)	subject of study	sociology, psychology
ics (noun, singular)	subject of study	economics, politics
less (adjective)	without	useless, endless
ly	makes an adverb from an adjective	quickly, happily
ness	makes an abstract noun from an adjective	happiness, sadness
y	makes an adjective from a noun	sandy, sunny

He's a hard **worker**. He works 12 hours a day.
She's a very good **swimmer**. She was on the
    Olympic team.
Her tennis is much better now that she has a new
    instructor.
The new **photocopier** makes very clear copies.
I use a **word processor** to write all my letters.

Thanks for the information. It was very **useful**.
What a **beautiful** photo. I think it will win first prize in the contest.

Studying **sociology** teaches you about society.
Studying **psychology** teaches you about people.

Economics is the study of money and finance.
He is a very good senator, though he has never studied **politics**.

This book is no help at all – it's **useless**.
I can't finish this book – it's **endless**.

He was late for work, so he walked **quickly** to the train station.
The little child ran **happily** across the grass.

The mother was smiling with **happiness** as she
    held her baby in her arms.
They said good-bye with great **sadness**.

That beach is very popular with tourists
    because it is long and **sandy**.
It's a beautiful, **sunny** day – let's go to the beach.

Exercises

26.1   Which words from page 54 do these pictures illustrate?

1. a s*unny day*................   3. a golf i....................   5. a s.......................

2. He's smiling h...........   4. a w.........................   6. a u................. thing

26.2   Match the adjectives with the nouns in the box. Some adjectives go with more than one noun.

fast worker / fast car / fast swimmer

1. fast   3. beautiful   5. sunny   7. useful
2. useless   4. sandy   6. hard   8. endless

worker   beach   weather   car   idea   book   swimmer   smile   picture   fun

26.3   Match these books with their subjects – *sociology, psychology, economics,* or *politics.*

1. *The President and Congress in the U.S.*
2. *Japanese Society Today*
3. *The Future of Banking*
4. *Why People Smile*

26.4   Are there suffixes in your language? Write a translation or an explanation for the suffixes in the chart on page 54.

26.5   What do you think these words and phrases mean? Use the information about suffixes on page 54 to help you.

1. zoology   *the study of animals*   6. painless
2. a traveler   7. badly
3. slowly   8. a can opener
4. hopeful   9. mathematics
5. rainy   10. a surfer

Words you may confuse

A Similar sounds

quite/quiet
This book is **quite** good. /kwaɪt/ [fairly good / very good]
My bedroom is very **quiet**. /ˈkwaɪ.ət/ [silent / no noise]

lose/loose
A: Why do I always **lose** my keys? /luːz/
B: Here they are.

If you **lose** something, you do not
know where it is / you can't find it.

This ring is very **loose**. /luːs/ [**Loose** means
it is not tight, because it is too big.]

fell/felt
Fell is the past tense of **fall**.
   Yesterday I **fell** and broke my arm.

Felt is the past tense of **feel**.
   I **felt** sick yesterday, but I **feel** fine today.

B Similar or related meanings

*Do you want
to borrow it?*

lend/borrow
If you **lend** something, you *give* it.
If you **borrow** something, you *get/take* it.

Sam wants to use Rita's bicycle:
SAM: Will you **lend** me your bicycle?
   [You *give* it to me for a day / an hour.]
or Can I **borrow** your bicycle? [I *get* it from you.]
RITA: Yes, take it.
SAM: Thanks.

miss/lose
I got up late and **missed the bus / missed my class**.
   [You didn't do something that was planned.]
I **lost** my homework on the way to class.
   [You can't find it.]

C Other words often mixed up

The **afternoon** is from 12 noon until about
   5 or 6 p.m.
The **evening** is from 5 or 6 p.m. until about
   9 or 10 p.m.
After 9 or 10 p.m. it is the **night**.
I **hope** I pass my exams. [I really want to pass.]
I have not studied; I **expect** I'll fail my exams.
   [It's probable or likely.]

Exercises

27.1 Fill in the blanks with words from A on page 56. The first letter of the word is given.

1. Please be q*uiet*............. The baby is sleeping.
2. If you l.................. your passport, you have to call the embassy.
3. I f.................. tired this morning, but I am OK now.
4. She f.................. and broke her leg. She had to go to the hospital.
5. It's q.................. cold today. Brrrr!
6. These shoes are very l.................... I need smaller ones.

27.2 Circle the correct answer.

1. **Quite** has	a) one syllable	b) two syllables
2. **Quiet** has	a) one syllable	b) two syllables
3. The last sound of **loose** sounds like	a) *s*	b) *z*
4. The last sound of **lose** sounds like	a) *s*	b) *z*

27.3 Answer these questions.

1. If you want to use someone's camera for two hours, what do you say? Can I ..*borrow your camera?*.....................................
2. What do you say if someone makes too much noise? Please be ....
3. What do you say if you are going to a concert but can't find the tickets you bought? I've ....
4. What do you say to someone at 2 p.m.? Good ....
5. What do you say to a friend if you need 35 cents to make a phone call? Can you ....?
6. What do you say if you arrive at work late because your train left without you? Sorry I'm late – I ....

27.4 Answer these questions about *yourself.*

1. Are you expecting any visitors today?
2. What do you hope to do with this book?
3. Do you ever borrow things from your friends? What things?
4. Would you lend your best friend $500?
5. How do you feel today? How did you feel yesterday?

You can find other frequently confused words in these units in this book:

Do and **make**	Units 5 and 6
Take and **bring**	Units 8 and 9
Say and **tell**	Unit 13
Speak and **talk**	Unit 13
Rob and **steal**	Unit 57

Birth, marriage, and death

A Birth

Diana **had a baby** yesterday.
It **was born** at 1:15 yesterday morning.
It **weighed** 7 pounds.

They are going to **name/call** him John – after
John, his grandfather.
Grandfather John's **birthday** is June 16th too –
but he **was born** in 1953!
The baby's parents **were born** in 1980.

B Marriage

If you have a husband or wife, you are **married**.
If you are not married, you are **single**.
If her husband dies, a woman is a **widow**. If his wife dies, a man is a **widower**.
(You can also say you are **widowed**.)
If your marriage breaks up, you are **separated/divorced**.
(With **divorce**, the marriage has legally ended.)

The wedding

bride   (bride)groom

Bill and Sarah **got married**.
Sarah **got married** to Bill. (*not* ~~with~~ Bill)
They went to Italy on their **honeymoon**.
They **were married** for twenty years.

C Death

Then Bill **became ill**.
He **died** last year.
He **died of** a heart attack.
Bill is **dead**.
Sarah is a **widow**.

The funeral

Exercises

28.1 When and where were you and your family and friends born? Write sentences about five people.

My mother was born in Buenos Aires on July 4, 1955.

28.2 When were these people born and when did they die? Write sentences.

1. Christopher Columbus (1451–1506)
   Christopher Columbus was born in 1451 and died in 1506.
2. Diana, Princess of Wales (1961–1997)
3. Genghis Khan (1162–1227)
4. Elvis Presley (1935–1977)
5. Joan of Arc (1412–1431)
6. Martin Luther King, Jr. (1929–1968)

Elvis Presley (1935–1977)

28.3 Fill in the blanks with *died, dead,* or *death.*

1. Jill's grandfather .... last year.
2. His .... was a great shock to her.
3. Her grandmother has been .... for five years now.
4. She .... of a heart attack.
5. Now all Jill's grandparents are ....

28.4 Find a word or phrase on page 58 that means . . .

1. the name for a woman on her wedding day.   *bride*
2. the name for a man on his wedding day.
3. what you are if you have never been married.
4. to be 100 pounds.
5. what you are if your marriage has legally ended.
6. a ceremony, usually religious, after a person dies.
7. a vacation after a wedding.
8. what you are if your husband or wife dies.

28.5 Fill in the blanks with words from the box.

in	after	of	to	born	on

(1) .... 1997 Anne got married (2) .... Robert Smith. Unfortunately, Robert's grandmother, Rose Smith, died (3) .... a stroke soon after their wedding. Robert and Anne were (4) .... their honeymoon when she died. Their baby daughter was (5) .... two years later. They named the baby Rose, (6) .... Robert's grandmother.

28.6 Write about your family. Use words and expressions from page 58.

The family

Here is a **family tree** [a drawing that shows all the members of a family] for some of Anne and Paul Mason's **relatives** [people in their family].

William + Mary Mason

Henry + Diana

Carol   Anne + Paul   John   George + Sandra

Sarah   Jack   Emily   Peter

Paul is Anne's **husband** and Sarah and Jack's **father**.
Anne is Paul's **wife** and Sarah and Jack's **mother**.
Anne and Paul are Sarah and Jack's **parents**.
Sarah is Anne and Paul's **daughter**. Jack is their **son**.
Sarah is Jack's **sister**. Jack is Sarah's **brother**.
Henry is Sarah and Jack's **grandfather**. Diana is their **grandmother**.
Henry and Diana are Sarah and Jack's **grandparents**.
Sarah is Henry and Diana's **granddaughter**. Jack is their **grandson**.
John and George are Sarah and Jack's **uncles**.
Carol and Sandra are Sarah and Jack's **aunts**.
Sarah is Carol, John, George, and Sandra's **niece**. Jack is their **nephew**.
Emily and Peter are Sarah and Jack's **cousins**.

Exercises

29.1   **Look at the family tree on page 60. Complete the sentences.**

   1. Emily is Peter's ...*sister*.......
   2. Peter is Emily's ....
   3. Anne is Emily's ....
   4. Paul is Peter's ....
   5. Diana is Peter's ....
   6. Henry is Emily's ....
   7. Peter is Paul's ....
   8. Emily is Paul's ....
   9. Sandra is Emily's ....
  10. Sandra is George's ....
  11. Sarah is Peter's ....

29.2   **Draw your family tree. Then write about your relatives.**

Anne is my mother.

29.3   **The Masons have some other relatives. Complete the paragraph about them.**

 Laura   Howard

Sandra has a brother, Howard. Howard is Peter's (1) ...*uncle*......... Howard's wife is Emily's (2) .... They are all very good friends. But Henry has a sister, Laura. Henry is Laura's (3) .... Laura does not get along well with William, her (4) ...., but William loves Laura's three sons, who are his (5) .... Laura's boys are Paul's (6) ...., but they do not see each other very often. Then there is Anne's mother, Mrs. Scott. She is Sarah and Jack's (7) .... She and Anne, her (8) ...., like to play golf together.

29.4   **Ask a friend. Then write sentences about your friend's family.**
Chen has one brother and no sisters.

   1. Do you have any brothers and sisters?
   2. Do you have any cousins?
   3. Do you have any nieces or nephews?
   4. Do you have any grandparents?   *or*   Are any of your grandparents living?

29.5   **Cover page 60. How many family words can you write down in two minutes? Check what you wrote carefully against the book. Did you spell everything correctly? Which words did you forget?**

UNIT 30 Parts of the body

A Head and face

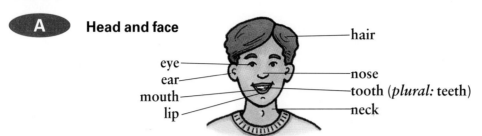

hair
eye
ear
mouth
lip
nose
tooth (*plural:* teeth)
neck

B Arm and leg

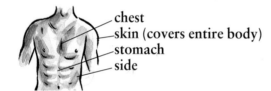

finger
nail
thumb
shoulder
arm
hand

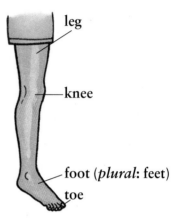

leg
knee
foot (*plural:* feet)
toe

C Rest of the body

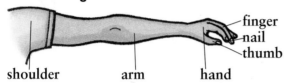

chest
skin (covers entire body)
stomach
side

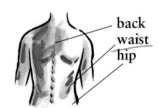

back
waist
hip

D Inside the body

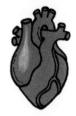 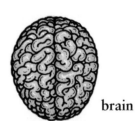

heart   brain   blood

E Pronunciation problems

See the chart of phonetic symbols on page 125 or check the dictionary for help:
eye /aɪ/   knee /ni/   stomach /ˈstʌmək/   heart /hɑrt/
blood /blʌd/   foot /fʊt/   tooth /tuθ/

F Grammar

Use *my, your, his, her*, etc., with parts of the body (usually).
Jane is washing **her** hair. (*not* Jane is washing ~~the~~ hair.)
I have a pain in **my** leg. (*not* I have a pain in ~~the~~ leg.)

Exercises

30.1 Complete these sentences with words from page 62.

1. A hand has five ..*fingers*.......
2. The .... is a symbol of love.
3. An adult has 32 ....
4. You smell with your ....
5. A foot has five ....
6. You hear with your ....
7. You use your .... to think!
8. Your .... type can be A, B, AB, or O.

30.2 Words for parts of the body are used in different contexts too. Look at the pictures below and answer the questions.

1.   a.
        b.

c. 2.

3.

5.

4.

1. A chair has arms, legs, and a back. Which letters do you think label these parts?
2. This is a needle. Where is its eye?
3. This is a clock. Where is its face? Where are its hands?
4. This is a bottle. Where is its neck?
5. This is a mountain. Where is its foot?

30.3 Parts of the body are often used in compound nouns too. Complete these nouns with a word from page 62.

1. ....*arm*chair   3. ....stick   5. ....ring

2. ....ball   4. ....brush   6. ....bag

30.4 Translate six words from page 62 into your own language, and write them down. Then pick six different words from page 62, and draw a picture of what each word means. Next week, test yourself. Which words do you remember best – the words you learned with a translation or with a picture?

A Clothes

hat · coat · jacket · scarf · gloves · shoes · boots · suit · socks · skirt · tie · T-shirt · shirt · dress · belt · sweater

B Plural words

These words are always plural in English. They need a plural verb.

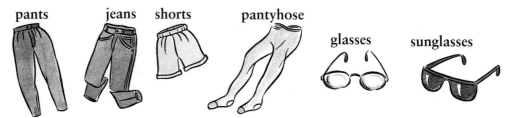

pants · jeans · shorts · pantyhose · glasses · sunglasses

My suit is new, but these pants are old. Her shorts/jeans/pantyhose are black.

Note: You say: a pair of shorts/glasses/pants, etc.

C Verbs

You **wear** clothes, but you **carry** things. (*not* you ~~use~~ clothes)
  Sue **is wearing** a long red coat. She's **carrying** a suitcase
    and a small handbag/purse.
  You can also say: Sue **has** a red coat **on**.
  You **carry** a briefcase and an umbrella.

In the morning you **get dressed** or **put** your
clothes **on**. At night you **get undressed** or
take your clothes **off**.

Tip: Can you name all the clothes you usually wear? If not, use a dictionary
to help you find the words you need.

Exercises

31.1 Put these words into one or both columns.

	men	*women*
coat jacket dress tie belt shoes suit skirt pantyhose shirt pants sweater T-shirt handbag briefcase	coat	coat

31.2 Match the part of the body with the item of clothing.

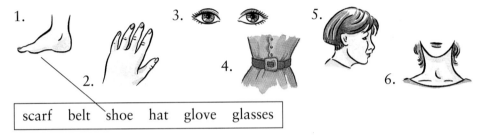

| scarf   belt   shoe   hat   glove   glasses |

31.3 Choose a verb from the box and put it in the correct form.

| be   wear   carry   have |

1. John's jeans ...*are*......... blue, and his T-shirt .... red.
2. Julia .... jeans and a T-shirt today.
3. Sarah .... a red coat on and she .... some flowers. Where is she going?
4. Siree's dress .... old, but her shoes .... new.
5. Last year Antonio's pants .... white. Now they .... gray.
6. .... this a new pair of jeans?

31.4 Look at the picture and write the names next to the numbers.

...*sunglasses*... 1.

.... 2.

.... 3.

.... 4.

.... 5.

6. ....

7. ....

8. ....

9. ....

10. ....

31.5 Write a paragraph about what you are wearing today.

I'm wearing a white T-shirt and a blue sweater. I have a pair of black pants on. I'm wearing blue socks and white shoes. I also have a pair of glasses on.

UNIT 32 Describing people

A Height [How many feet and inches *or* how many meters?]

Mary is a very **tall** woman. (*not* Mary is
a very ~~high~~ woman.) Tom is **short**. (*not*
Tom is ~~low~~.)
If you aren't tall or short, you are **medium height**.
To ask if someone is tall or short, you say:
  How tall is Mary/Tom?
    She's 5 foot 10 [5 feet and 10 inches tall] / 1.78 meters.
    He's 5 feet tall / 1.5 meters.

Mary   Tom

B Weight [How many pounds *or* kilos?]

Mee-sun is really **slim**.
I was very **thin** when I was in the hospital. (**Thin** is
  a more negative word.)
A **fat** man opened the door. (**Fat** is a
  negative word.)

Mee-sun

The doctor said I am **overweight**.
[more pounds/kilos than is good for me]

How much do you weigh?
  I weigh 154 pounds / 70 kilos.

C Face and head

Sally has **dark** hair and **dark skin**.
  She has **brown** eyes.
Liz has **blonde** hair and **light/fair skin**.
  She has **blue** eyes.
Bill has **a beard** and **a mustache** and **long** hair.
  He has **green** eyes.
Taka has **short black** hair.

Sally   Liz

Bill   Taka

D Age

My great-grandmother is 97. She's very **old**. My sister is 14. She's **young** but
would like to be **older**. My father is 50. He's **middle-aged** but would like to be
younger!

This nursing home is for **elderly** people. (more polite than **old**)

E Looks: positive (+) and negative (−)

My sister is very **pretty**. (+) (usually girls/women only).
  She's a **beautiful** girl. (+)
Jim's a very **handsome** man. (+) (usually for boys/men only)
  Bob is **unattractive/ugly**. (−)
I'm not ugly or beautiful. I'm just **average / ordinary-looking**! (+/−)

66

Exercises

32.1 Fill in the blanks with words from page 66.

1. He's only 4 foot 11. He's kind of ...*short*........ .
2. Very .... people are often good at basketball.
3. Models are usually ....
4. Is her skin dark? No, it's ....
5. She's only 12. She's still ....
6. If I eat too much, I'll be ....
7. My grandmother lives in this home. It's a home for .... people.
   (Don't use "old.")

32.2 Ask questions for these answers. Use the words in parentheses.

1. ...*How tall is your brother*......? (your brother)
   He's about 5 foot 9.
2. Is ....? (Elena's hair)
   No, her hair's dark.
3. Is ....? (Mike's hair)
   Yes, it is fairly long.
4. Are ....? (your parents)
   Not really, they're middle-aged.
5. Why ....? (Hiromi – thin)
   She's been very sick recently.

32.3 Write sentences describing the people in these pictures.

Sue   Jeff   Wendy   Dick

1. Sue has ....
2. Jeff has ....
3. Wendy has ....
4. Dick's hair is ...., and he ....

32.4 Write down the names of three people you know. Then write about:

– their height (tall, short, medium height)
– their hair (color, long, short, beard)
– their eyes (color)
– their looks (average, handsome, etc.)

UNIT 33 Health and illness

A   How are you today?

I'm **fine**, thanks. / I am **very well**, thanks.
I **don't feel very well**. I have to go home and rest. (I'll probably be OK
  tomorrow.)
I **feel sick/ill**. Can you call **a doctor**? (possibly a serious problem)
That fish was bad. I think I'm going to be **sick** / I'm going to **throw up**! [**vomit**]

B   Everyday problems

I **have a headache**. Have you got **an aspirin**?

I **have a toothache**. I need to go to the dentist.

I'm going to bed with some hot tea. I **have a cold**.
(See Unit 3.)

C   Problems people have for many years / all their lives

I get **allergies** every summer, from
flowers and grass. I **sneeze** all day.

sneeze

My little brother has **asthma**;
sometimes he can't breathe.

D   Illnesses in hot/tropical countries

mosquito

In some places, mosquitoes can give people **malaria**.
The drinking water was bad, and many children had **cholera**. [a disease caused
  by bacteria in the drinking water]

E   Serious illnesses

My father **had a heart attack**.
  He is **in the hospital**.
Every year **cancer** kills many
  people who smoke.

F   How to stay fit and healthy

Eat a good **diet**: Eat lots of fruits and vegetables.
Get some exercise: Swimming, jogging, and cycling are good for you.
Don't have too much **stress**: Relax after work or class.
  Don't panic about work!

68

Exercises

33.1   Put these health problems in the three columns. Do you think they are *not very serious, somewhat serious,* or *very serious*?

cancer   a toothache   cholera   allergies   a headache
a heart attack   a cold   asthma   malaria

Not very serious	*Somewhat serious*	*Very serious*
a headache		

33.2   Complete the conversations.

  1. A: How are you today?
     B: ....
     A: Good!

  2. A: Are you OK?
     B: No, ...
     A: Would you like a glass of water?
     B: Yes, thank you.

  3. A: I ....
     B: Should I call a doctor?
     A: Yes, I think so.

  4. A: ....
     B: Here's the phone number of a good dentist.
     A: Thanks.

  5. A: Your nose is red. Do you have ....?
     B: Yes.
     A: Why don't you have a hot drink and go to bed early?

33.3   Answer these questions about yourself. Use a dictionary if you need to.

  1. What do you think is a good diet?
  2. What kind of exercise do you like?
  3. Do you have a lot of stress in your life?
  4. Have you ever been in the hospital?

33.4   What illnesses are connected with . . .

  1. a mosquito bite?   *malaria*
  2. bad drinking water?
  3. pollution, traffic fumes?
  4. grass, flowers, etc.?
  5. smoking?

UNIT 34 Feelings

A Love/like/hate

love   like   don't like   hate
                                 (dislike)

I **love** my family and my best friend.
I **like** my job.
I **don't like** horror movies. "I **dislike** horror movies" is less common.
I **hate** traffic jams.
I **prefer** coffee **to** tea. [I like coffee more than I like tea.]
I **want** [I would like] **a new car.** (**want** + noun)
I **want to buy** a new car. (**want** + infinitive)
Note: I **want my father to buy** a new car. (**want** + object + infinitive)
   (*not* ~~I want that~~ . . .)
I **hope to do** well on my exams. (**hope** + infinitive)
I **hope** (**that**) my friend does well on his exams. (**hope** + *that* clause)

B Happy/sad/tired

happy   sad   upset

angry   surprised   tired

hungry   sick/ill   cold

thirsty   warm   hot

Exercises

34.1   **Do you love, like, not like, or hate these things? Write sentences.**

1. chocolate   *I love chocolate.*
2. cowboy movies (westerns)
3. airplanes
4. tea
5. soccer
6. cats
7. cars
8. jazz

34.2   **Which do you prefer? Write answers as in the example.**

1. tea or coffee?   *I prefer coffee to tea.*
2. dogs or cats?
3. shopping or sightseeing?
4. Toyotas or Fords?
5. strawberry or chocolate ice cream?
6. watching sports or playing sports?

34.3   **Answer these questions using *want* or *hope*.**

1. You're thirsty. What do you want?   *I want something to drink.*
2. The lesson feels very long. What do you hope?
3. You're hungry. What do you want?
4. Your friend is sick. What do you hope?
5. You're tired. What do you want?
6. You haven't seen your best friend in months. What do you hope?

34.4   **Look at the pictures. How do these people feel? Use words from B on page 70.**

1. Marie *is hungry*..............

4. Bob..............

2. Fred ....

5. Mr. Lee..............

3. The children ....

6. Mrs. Jones..............

34.5   **When did you last feel . . .**

1. angry?   2. surprised?   3. upset?
I felt angry this morning when I read the newspaper.

Greetings and other useful phrases

A Every day

Good morning. Good afternoon. Good evening.

When you leave someone, usually you both say **Goodbye** or maybe **See you soon** or **Take care!** (informal)

When someone goes to bed, you usually say **Good night**. You can also say **Sleep well.** Don't say **Good night** when you arrive somewhere, only when you leave (at night).

If you ask for something, you often say **Please**.

If someone does something nice for you, you say **Thank you** or **Thanks**.

B Special days

If someone is going to do something difficult (e.g., take an exam or have a job interview), you say **Good luck!**

If someone has done something special (e.g., done well on an exam, gotten a new job, had a baby) you say **Congratulations!**

When it is someone's birthday, you say **Happy Birthday.** (*not* ~~Congratulations~~)

On (or just after) January 1st (New Year's Day), you say **Happy New Year.**

Exercises

35.1 Choose phrases from page 72 to fit the conversations.

1. A: *(sneezes)* Atchoo!
   B: ...*Bless you.*......................

2. A: I'm taking my driving test today.
   B: ....

3. A: I passed my driving test!
   B: ....

4. A: Good-bye.
   B: ....

5. A: It's my birthday today.
   B: ....

6. A: How are you?
   B: ....

7. A: Hello!
   B: ....

8. A: Here's your coffee.
   B: ....

35.2 What is the person saying in each picture?

35.3 What do you say? Choose a phrase from page 72.

1. You want to order a sandwich. The waiter is reading the newspaper.
   Excuse me.
2. A child says "Good night" to you.
3. You answer the phone at work. It is 10:30 a.m.
4. It is 2 a.m. on January 1st. You meet a friend on the street.
5. A friend spoke too quickly. You didn't understand.

35.4 Ann and Bill meet in a cafe. Bill usually says the wrong thing.
Correct his mistakes.

ANN: Hi.
BILL: Good night.
ANN: How are you?
BILL: Terrible. I have a bad cold and . . .
ANN: It's my birthday today.
BILL: Good luck!

ANN: Would you like something to drink?
BILL: No, thank you. A diet soda.
ANN: With ice?
BILL: No, please.
ANN: Here you are.
BILL: Bless you!

35.5 Write a conversation using phrases from page 72. Use as many as possible.

Countries, languages, and people

All the nouns and adjectives in this unit always begin with a capital letter, e.g., Africa (*not* africa) and Spanish (*not* spanish).

A Continents and countries

The names of the continents are marked in blue. It is not possible to show all the countries of the world on this page. If your country is not included, check its English name with your teacher or in a reference book such as an atlas.

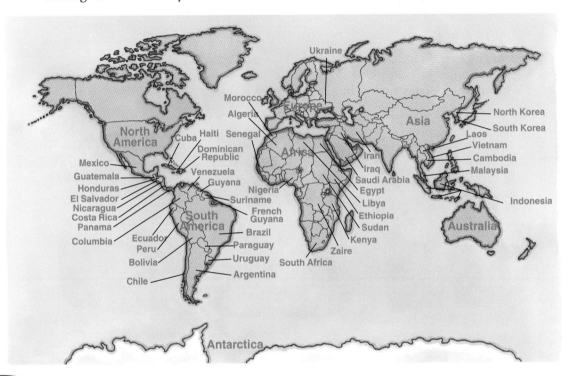

B People

Adjectives of nationality describe people from different countries, groups, or regions (e.g., a Brazilian man, a Korean woman, a Mexican family, etc.).

With -an or -ian:	Mexican, Canadian, Korean, Russian, Australian, Chilean, Brazilian, Indonesian, Egyptian, Peruvian, Venezuelan, Italian
With -ish:	Spanish, British, Polish, Turkish, Irish, Swedish, Danish
With -ese:	Chinese, Portuguese, Japanese, Vietnamese, Taiwanese
Exceptions:	French (from France), Dutch (from Holland), Swiss (from Switzerland), Filipino (from the Philippines), Thai, Greek, Iraqi, Arab, Israeli

C Languages and people

Words for languages are usually the same as the adjective of nationality: **English, Chinese, Spanish, Japanese, Thai, French, Korean, Portuguese**, etc. An exception is **Arabic** (the language).

Exercises

You may need to use a reference book to help you with some of these exercises
– it is not possible to include every country and nationality on page 74.

36.1 **In which continents are these places?**

1. Mount Everest *Asia*
2. the Alps
3. the Amazon River
4. the Great Barrier Reef
5. the Great Wall
6. the Andes Mountains
7. the Nile River
8. Mount Fuji
9. the Grand Canyon

36.2 **Match these capital cities with their countries.**

1. Tokyo
2. Beijing
3. Seoul
4. Bogotá
5. Caracas
6. Washington, D.C.
7. Bangkok
8. Buenos Aires
9. Rome
10. Mexico City

a. Thailand
b. Italy
c. Mexico
d. China
e. Japan
f. Argentina
g. South Korea
h. Colombia
i. the United States
j. Venezuela

36.3 **Write down in English . . .**

1. the name of your country.
2. the names of the countries next to your country.
3. the word for your language.
4. the name for people from your country.

36.4 **Which country is different? (Think of the languages they speak there.) Write sentences.**

1. England, Canada, Russia, Australia   *In England, Canada, and Australia they speak English, but in Russia they speak Russian.*
2. Mexico, Brazil, Spain, Panama
3. Italy, Austria, Germany, Switzerland
4. Taiwan, Japan, China, Singapore

36.5 **What is the adjective for these countries?**

1. Cuba *Cuban*
2. Thailand
3. Egypt
4. Brazil
5. Canada
6. Mexico
7. the Philippines
8. France
9. Peru
10. China
11. Vietnam
12. Indonesia
13. Chile

UNIT 37 Weather

A   Types of weather

sun    rain   clouds   snow

fog

wind

thunder

lightning

B   Nouns, adjectives, and verbs

Noun	Adjective
sun	sunny
rain	rainy
wind	windy
cloud	cloudy
snow	snowy
fog	foggy
thunder	–
lightning	–

It's a **sunny** day in Tokyo today, but it's **cloudy** in Hong Kong.
It's **foggy** in Vancouver, and it's **snowing** / it's **snowy** in Ottawa.
It's **raining** in São Paulo, but **the sun is shining** in Rio de Janeiro.
It's **beautiful** weather today. (*not* It's a beautiful weather.)
The weather is **awful** today.

You cannot say: It's ~~winding/clouding/fogging/sunning~~.

C   Other weather words

It is very **hot** in Mexico – sometimes more than **100 degrees Fahrenheit** in summer.
It is very **cold** in the Arctic – it is often **minus 50 degrees Celsius** there.
It is often **wet** in Seattle – carry an umbrella when you go sightseeing there.
It is very **dry** in the Sahara – it doesn't rain much there.
A **hurricane** is an extremely strong wind.
A **storm** is when there is a strong wind and rain together.
A **thunderstorm** is when there is thunder, lightning, rain, and sometimes wind together.

Tip: If you are able to see the weather forecast in English on TV, watch it as often as you can.

76

Exercises

37.1 Match the words and the symbols.

1. snow   2. sun   3. rain   4. fog   5. lightning   6. wind   7. clouds

a.   b.   c.   d.

e.   f.   g.

37.2 Look at the types of weather in A on page 76. Write them down in order from your most favorite to your least favorite.

37.3 Write sentences about the places in the chart.

Bangkok   1. It is .....*sunny in Bangkok*.. .

Taipei   2. It is .....*raining in Taipei*.. .

Caracas   3. It is ....

London   4. ....

Seoul   5. ....

Toronto   6. ....

37.4 Complete these sentences with a word from page 76.

1. The sun was ...*shining*...... this morning.
2. When it ...., I take my umbrella.
3. It is beautiful .... today.
4. It is .... now; maybe we can go skiing.
5. You see .... before you hear thunder.
6. It is dangerous to be in a small boat at sea in a ....

37.5 Are these sentences true about the weather in your country? If not, correct them.

1. It often snows in December.
2. It is usually 80 degrees Fahrenheit in summer and 0 degrees Fahrenheit in winter.
3. There are thunderstorms every day in August.
4. It is very wet in spring.
5. We never have hurricanes.
6. Summer is my favorite season because it is usually hot and dry.

37.6 Write about the weather where you are today. Use as many words as possible from page 76.

UNIT 38 In the city

A Downtown

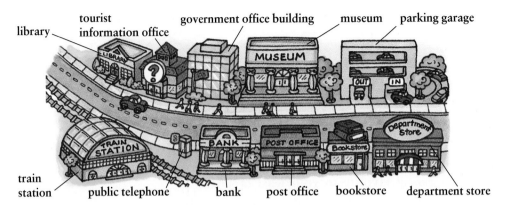

library — tourist information office — government office building — museum — parking garage

train station — public telephone — bank — post office — bookstore — department store

You can **get/take a train** at the **train station**.
You can **change money** at the **bank**.
You can **read books** and **newspapers** at the **library**.
You can **buy books** at a **bookstore**.
You can **park your car** in/at the **parking garage**.

B Streets and roads

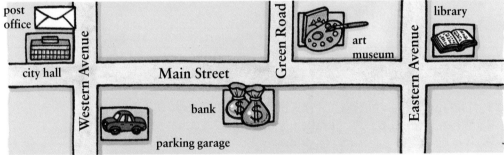

post office — city hall — Western Avenue — Main Street — bank — parking garage — Green Road — art museum — Eastern Avenue — library

Asking for help
Where is city hall? **How do I get to** X street? **Is there** a public telephone nearby? **Can I park** here? **Excuse me, I'm looking for** the museum.

C People in the city

police officer   taxi driver   salesclerk   librarian   bank teller

D Signs

no parking   no entry   bus stop   railroad crossing   signal ahead

78

Exercises

38.1 **Answer the questions about A on page 78.**

1. Where can I get a train to New York?   *At the train station.*
2. Where can I get information about hotels?
3. Where can I change money?
4. Where can I park?
5. Where can I see paintings?
6. Where can I mail a letter?
7. Where can I buy a book?
8. Where can I read (or borrow) a book, without buying it?

38.2 **Look at the map in B on page 78. Ask questions.**

1. *Where's the library?*   On Eastern Avenue, near Main Street.
2. ....   It's next to City Hall.
3. ....   Go right on Green Road.
4. ....   The garage on Western Avenue is best.
5. ....   There's a bank on Main Street.

38.3 **Where do these people work?**

1. bus driver   *on a bus*
2. salesclerk
3. librarian
4. police officer
5. bank teller

38.4 **What are these signs?**

1. ....   2. ....   3. ....   4. ....   5. ....

38.5 **Write a paragraph about your city or town. Use words from page 78.**

UNIT 39 In the country

The **country** (or the **countryside**) means "outside of cities or towns" and often includes farmland. **Country** can also mean a nation (e.g., Brazil, Japan, Italy).

A Things you can see in the country

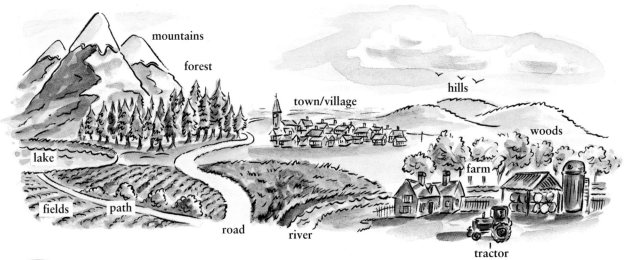

B Living and working in the country

In the country, many people live in a **town** [an area smaller than a city] or a **village** [smaller than a town].
A **farmer** lives **on a farm** and works in the **fields**.
My friend lives in a **cabin**. [a small, simple house in the country or mountains]

C Nature

Nature means "everything in the natural world" (e.g., animals, birds, plants).
I love **nature**. (*not* I love ~~the~~ nature.)
I like walking **in the country**. (*not* I like walking in the ~~nature~~. "Nature" is not a place.)
Animals, birds, fish, and insects that live away from people are called **wildlife**.
There is wonderful **wildlife** in the north of the country.

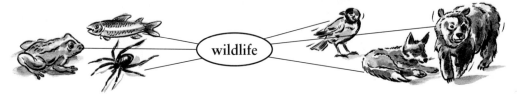

Conservation is the protection of animals, plants, and natural areas from damage (e.g., **wildlife conservation**).

80

Exercises

39.1 Cover page 80. How many names of things in the country can you remember?

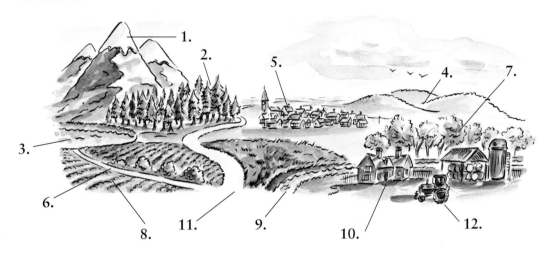

39.2 Fill in the blanks.

1. My brother is a ..*farmer*....... . He lives .... a farm.
2. It's not a big house; it's just a ....
3. The farm is near a small ....; a few hundred people live there.
4. We like to climb the .... near our home.
5. We went swimming in a .... near the farm. The water was warm.
6. There is some wonderful .... in this area, especially birds.
7. Let's go for a walk along the .... It goes through the woods and fields and down to the lake.

39.3 Describe the typical countryside where you come from. Write at least four sentences about it. Use these questions to help you.

1. Are there any woods or forests?
2. Are there any hills or mountains?
3. Are there any lakes or rivers?
4. Are there many small towns or villages?
5. Are there farms?
6. Are there paths where you can walk?
7. Can you see wildlife?

39.4 Put *the* in the sentence if necessary.

1. He loves .... nature.
2. She wants to live in .... country.
3. They are interested in .... wildlife.

Animals and pets

A Farm animals

Animal	Baby	Meat	Other products
cow	calf	beef, veal (from a calf)	leather, milk
sheep	lamb	lamb (from a lamb)	wool
pig	piglet	pork, bacon, ham	
chicken	chick	chicken	eggs

B Wild or zoo animals

C Pets

These animals are often **pets** [animals that people keep in their homes].

Parrots and parakeets are **birds**.
You **take** your dog **for a walk,** but you don't usually take your cat for a walk.

Exercises

40.1 Complete these sentences with words from page 82.

1. A ..*turtle*.. moves very slowly.
2. A .... has a very long neck.
3. ...., ..., and .... are birds.
4. .... and .... are large cats.
5. You can ride a .... and an ....
6. .... swim and .... fly.
7. You can buy .... at a butcher shop or a supermarket.
8. .... and .... give us food for breakfast.

40.2 Match the animal with its meat. Draw lines.

Animal	Meat
1. chicken	a. lamb
2. calf	b. ham
3. lamb	c. beef
4. cow	d. chicken
5. pig	e. veal

40.3 Look at the animals on page 82. Which of them . . .

1. eat meat?
2. give us things that we wear?
3. produce their babies in eggs?

40.4 Look at the pictures and complete the crossword puzzle.

40.5 There are seventeen different animals in the pictures on page 82. Cover the page. How many of these animals can you remember?

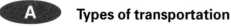

UNIT 41 Travel

A Types of transportation

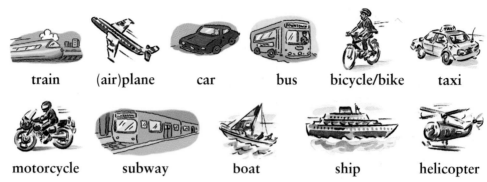

train   (air)plane   car   bus   bicycle/bike   taxi

motorcycle   subway   boat   ship   helicopter

B Useful travel words

map   schedule   customs   luggage   passport

Can I have a **one-way / round-trip** ticket to Chicago, please?
   (one-way = Toronto → Chicago; round-trip = Toronto → Chicago → Toronto)
How much is the train/bus/taxi/air **fare**?
Was it a long **trip**? (*not* Was it a long ~~travel~~?)

C By train

The train **arriving at** Platform 3 is the 4:50
   train to Washington, D.C.
The Philadelphia train **departs/leaves from**
   Platform 6.
Is there a **dining car** on this train? [a special car where passengers can eat]
Do I have to **change trains**? [get off one train and get onto another]

D By plane

You have to **check in** [tell the airline that you are in the airport] an hour before
   the plane **takes off** [leaves the ground].
You can **check your luggage** before the flight. [Your luggage is taken on the
   plane.] After you arrive, you pick up your luggage at the **baggage claim** area.
Give your **boarding pass** to an airline employee when you get on the plane.
   [card that passengers need to get on a plane]
Have a good **flight**. [trip on an airplane]
The plane **landed** in Chicago at 5:30. [arrived]

E By car

We **rented a car** for a week. We had to **fill** it **up with gas**.
I'm going into town. Can I **give** you **a ride/lift**? [take
   someone in your car]

Exercises

41.1 Match the words on the left with their definitions on the right. Draw lines.

1. land
2. fare
3. dining car
4. ship
5. schedule
6. platform
7. luggage

a. a place to eat on a train
b. bags and suitcases
c. it says when trains depart and arrive
d. what you pay for travel
e. when a plane arrives at an airport
f. it travels on water, e.g., the *Titanic*
g. where you stand when you are waiting for a train

41.2 Can you answer these questions about travel?

1. What is the difference between a one-way ticket and a round-trip ticket?
2. What do you get at the baggage claim area of an airport?
3. Does a plane take off at the end of a trip? (If not, what does it do?)
4. What is the difference between renting a car and buying a car?
5. If you ask someone for a lift, do you want to go to the top floor?

41.3 Here are instructions to get to John's house from the airport.

When you arrive at the airport, take a number 10 bus to the train station. Then take a train to Centerville. The trip takes half an hour and you get off the train at the second stop. Take a taxi from the station to John's house.

Now write instructions for someone to get to your house from the airport or a train station.

41.4 Complete the crossword puzzle.

Across
3.
7.
9.

Down
1.
2.
4.
5.
6.
8.

Signs and notices

No smoking here.

You go in here.

You go out here.

There are lots of different signs for public bathrooms (toilets).

Men   Women

Restrooms   Gentlemen   Ladies

Tip: Look for other signs in English. Write down any that you see.

Exercises

42.1   Choose the correct letter.

1. Your sister wants to go to the restroom.
2. Your father wants to go to the restroom.
3. You want to go out of the store.
4. You want to pay for something.

42.2   Look at each of the signs and notices on page 86. Write down a place where you can see each of them.

No smoking – in a restaurant

42.3   Look at the pictures and answer the questions.

1. Can you go in now?   *No*   4. How do you open the door – A or B?

2. Can you use the telephone now?   5. How do you open the door – A or B?

3. Can you park your car here?   6. Is this a good time to go shopping?

42.4   Put the signs and notices on page 86 into two columns – *Information* (e.g., that a store is closed) and *Instructions* (e.g., that smoking is not allowed).

UNIT
43 Food and drink

A Everyday food

Would you like some **bread**?
   (*not* Would you like ~~a~~ bread?)
In Asia, many people eat **rice**.
Spaghetti is a type of **pasta**.
Some people eat **meat** or **fish** every day.
What would you like **for dessert, ice cream** or **cake**?

B Fast food

Fast food is often hot food, prepared and served quickly in informal restaurants (called fast-food restaurants). Some popular fast foods are:

hamburger	french fries	hot dog	pizza

Sometimes fast food is called **junk food** because it's not always good for you. (**Junk** can mean anything that is useless or of low quality.)

C Fruits and vegetables

carrots	green beans	potatoes	tomatoes	peas	onions	garlic	mushrooms

orange	apple	banana	pear	grapes	strawberries	pineapple

D Drinks

coffee	tea	milk	juice	soda/pop	mineral water / sparkling water

---

Tip: Go to a supermarket or grocery store. How many foods and drinks have English names on them? Try to learn some of them.

88

Exercises

43.1   Complete the sentences with words from A and B on page 88.

1. ..Rice......... is an important food in Japan.
2. French fries are made from ....
3. Macaroni, spaghetti, and linguini are all types of ....
4. Hamburgers are made from ....
5. Ice cream and cake are popular types of ....
6. Hamburgers, hot dogs, and fries are sometimes called ....

43.2   Put these words into two lists: fruits and vegetables. Then add two more items to each list.

| green bean   pineapple   carrot   grapes   onion |
| orange   banana   garlic   pear   mushroom |

Fruits	*Vegetables*
pineapple	

43.3   Write the names of these fruits and vegetables.

1. ....   2. ....   3. ....   4. ....   5. ....

43.4   There are six drinks in the puzzle. Can you find them?

```
A  J  A  N  O  W  S
J  U (S  O  D  A) I
M  I  L  K  A  T  T
U  C  O  F  F  E  E
T  E  M  L  O  R  A
```

43.5   What are your three favorite foods and your three favorite drinks? Which ones are good for you? Use a dictionary if you need to.

In the kitchen

A What's in the kitchen?

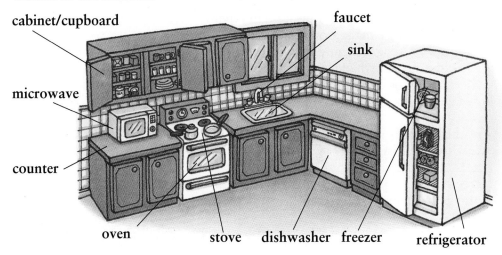

cabinet/cupboard
faucet
sink
microwave
counter
oven   stove   dishwasher   freezer   refrigerator

B Things you use in the kitchen

dishwashing liquid   pot   paper towels

dishtowel   frying pan   teapot   coffeemaker

C Things you use for eating and drinking

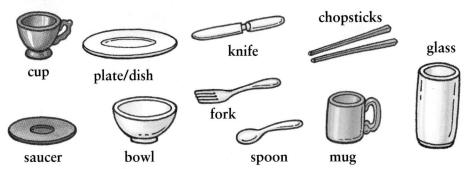

cup   plate/dish   knife   chopsticks   glass

saucer   bowl   fork   spoon   mug

D Questions in the kitchen

Where can I find a mug / a dishtowel / some paper towels?
Can I help with the dishes / the cooking?
Where does this cup / dish / frying pan **go**? (Where do you keep it?)
Where should I put this cup / the sugar?

Exercises

44.1

Check (✓) *yes* or *no*.	*yes*	*no*
1. I use a frying pan to drink out of.		✓
2. Dishwashing liquid makes the dishes clean.		
3. The refrigerator is cold inside.		
4. The freezer is not as cold as the refrigerator.		
5. I turn on the faucet to get water.		
6. A dishtowel is for making plates wet.		

44.2 Ask questions for these answers. Use words from page 90.

Where can I find the . . . ?

1. ....   It's in the cabinet.
2. ....   It's on the stove.
3. ....   Please put it in the sink.
4. ....   Thanks. You rinse off those plates, and I'll
put them in the dishwasher.

44.3 What do you need?

1. To make coffee I need .. *coffee, water, a coffeemaker, a cup, a spoon* .....
2. To make tea I need ....
3. To fry an egg I need ....
4. To eat my food I need ....
5. To drink some water I need ....
6. To make/cook my dinner in just two minutes I need ....

44.4 Look at the picture and answer the questions.

1. What's near the stove?   4. What's in the cabinet?
2. What's on the stove?   5. What's in the refrigerator?
3. What's in the freezer?   6. What's on the counter, near the microwave?

UNIT 45 In the bedroom and bathroom

A Bedroom

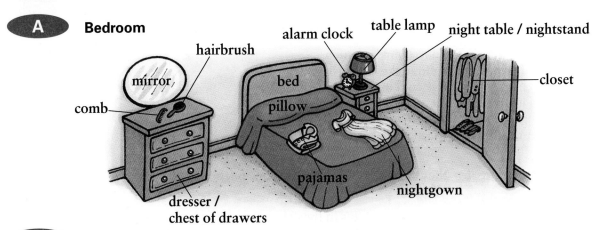

- alarm clock
- table lamp
- night table / nightstand
- hairbrush
- mirror
- bed
- closet
- comb
- pillow
- pajamas
- nightgown
- dresser / chest of drawers

B Bathroom

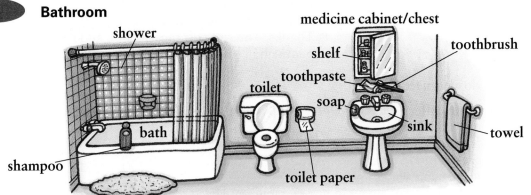

- shower
- medicine cabinet/chest
- shelf
- toothbrush
- toothpaste
- toilet
- soap
- bath
- sink
- towel
- shampoo
- toilet paper

C Joe's routine

Joe usually goes to bed at 11 o'clock.
He gets undressed and gets into bed.
He reads for a little while. Then he turns off the light and falls asleep.
He wakes up when his alarm clock rings.
He gets up and goes to the bathroom.
He brushes his teeth and takes a shower.
He gets dressed and goes to the kitchen for breakfast.
(See Unit 12.)

Exercises

45.1 Look at the picture and write the words next to the numbers.

45.2 Write down five more things that you need to take with you if you go to stay with a friend for one night.

.. **toothbrush** ....

....

45.3 Look at the pictures. Describe what the people are doing.

1. Anne ... *is brushing her teeth* ......   4. Mr. Park ....

2. Aya ....   5. James ....

3. Mr. and Mrs. Park ....   6. Antonio ....

45.4 Write down the words for all the things you have in your bathroom. Use a dictionary if you need to.

45.5 Describe your bedroom. Write four or five sentences.

45.6 Write about your nighttime and morning routines. Use the verbs in C on page 92. *I usually go to bed at . . .*

In the living room

A Things in the living room

bookcase | books | picture | phone book | phone | sofa/couch | curtains | light switch | stereo | TV/television | electrical outlet | CD player | armchair | end table | coffee table | carpet | chair

B Useful prepositions

The sofa is **near** the window.
The sofa is **next to** an end table.
The TV is **in the corner**.

The coffee table is **in the middle of** the room.
The bookcase is **against** the wall.
Where's the stereo?
    Under the TV.

C Things you do in the living room

Every evening I **watch TV**.
Sometimes I **listen to the radio** or **listen to music**.
Sometimes I **read**.
Sometimes I just **relax**. [rest and do nothing]

D Things you use

Where is **the remote control / remote** for the TV?
There's **a reading lamp** on the desk.
Close the curtains and **turn/switch on the light**; it's getting dark.
Please **turn off the radio** and **turn on the TV.** I want to watch the news.

Exercises

46.1   Write the names of . . .

1. somewhere you can put books.   *a bookcase*
2. somewhere two or three people can sit.
3. somewhere you can put down your coffee cup.
4. something you can look at on the wall.
5. something for turning the light on or off.
6. something for listening to music.
7. something under your feet.

46.2   Choose (a), (b), or (c).

1. If you want to lie back and relax, which is the best?
   (a) a chair   (b) an armchair   (c) a sofa
2. If it is dark and you want to read, do you . . .
   (a) close the curtains?   (c) turn off the light?
   (b) switch on the reading lamp?
3. If you want to watch a different TV station, do you . . .
   (a) use the remote control?   (c) turn off the TV?
   (b) use the electrical outlet?

46.3   Fill in the blanks with the correct prepositions. Look at the picture of the living room on page 94.

1. ...*On*.... the floor there is a carpet.
2. There is a small table .... the corner. There is a phone .... the table.
3. The TV is .... the sofa.
4. The bookcase is .... the wall.
5. The coffee table is .... front .... the sofa.

46.4   Write a paragraph about your living room at home. Draw a picture of it first. Describe your furniture (tables, chairs, sofa, etc.). Say where things are (e.g., next to . . . , in the corner . . . , near . . . , etc.). What color are the walls? Are there any pictures on them? What do you do when you are in your living room?

46.5   How many names of things in the living room can you find in the puzzle?

t	e	n	b	w	o
a	c	h	a	i	r
b	a	x	b	n	r
l	r	c	o	d	a
e	p	v	o	o	d
m	e	s	k	w	i
h	t	v	s	u	o

UNIT 47 Jobs

A What's his/her job?

doctor teacher nurse lawyer mechanic

secretary salesclerk hairdresser/hairstylist farmer

B Job (noun) and work (verb)

What's your **job**?   *or*   What **do** you **do**?
    I'm a waiter. / I'm a waitress.
Where do you **work**?
    I work in a restaurant.
Is it an interesting **job**?
    Yes, I like it.

C Workplaces

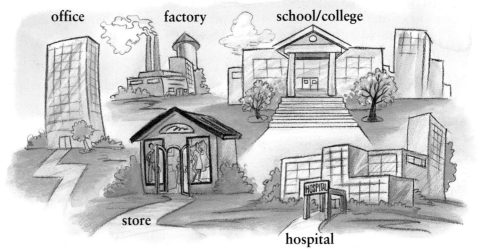

office   factory   school/college

store

hospital

I work **in** a factory / an office.
I work **at/from** home.

96

Exercises

47.1   **Where do they work?**

1. A teacher *works in a school/college/university* ....
2. A doctor ....
3. A waiter ....
4. A secretary ....
5. A salesclerk ....
6. A farmer ....

47.2   **Match the pictures with the jobs in the box.**

| farmer   lawyer   taxi driver   mechanic   nurse   secretary |

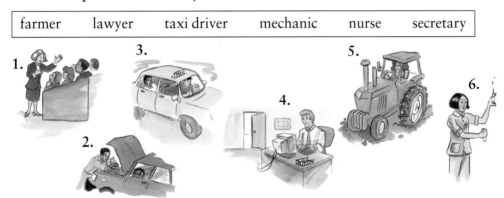

47.3   **Answer the questions about *yourself*. If you don't have a job, give answers about a friend or family member.**

1. What do you do?
2. Where do you work?
3. Is it an interesting job?

47.4   **Fill in the letters in the crossword puzzle.**

Across
1. works on a bus
2. works in a school
3. writes books

Down
1. works in a hospital
2. works in a restaurant
3. works with the doctor

School and university

A Subjects

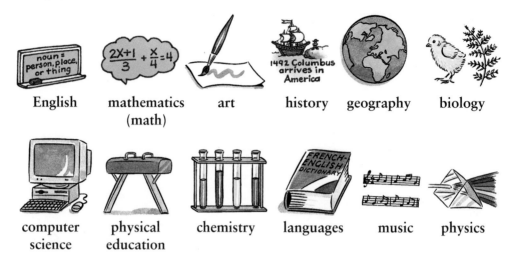

English | mathematics (math) | art | history | geography | biology

computer science | physical education | chemistry | languages | music | physics

B Useful things

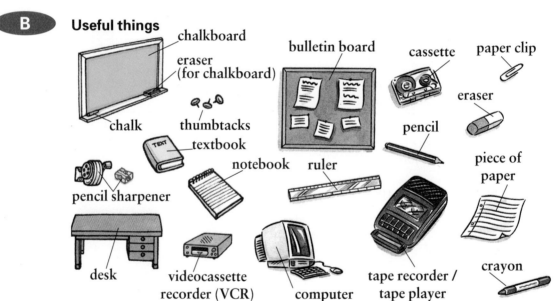

chalkboard
eraser (for chalkboard)
chalk
thumbtacks
textbook
pencil sharpener
notebook
desk
videocassette recorder (VCR)
computer
bulletin board
ruler
cassette
paper clip
eraser
pencil
piece of paper
tape recorder / tape player
crayon

C Useful verbs

A math teacher **teaches** math. His/Her students **study** math.
After school, students **do** their **homework**.
In elementary school, children **learn** to read and write.
A university teacher/professor **gives a lecture**, and the students **take notes**.
Students **take courses** in colleges and schools. At the end of a course, you often have to **take an exam.** You hope to **pass** your **exams.** You don't want to **fail** your **exams.**
If you complete your courses and pass the exams at a university, you **get a degree.**

Bachelor of Arts
Awarded to
David Lee
by
West College

Exercises

48.1 Match the subjects on the left with the examples on the right.

1. math
2. physics
3. history
4. geography
5. physical education
6. English
7. chemistry
8. biology
9. computer science

a. animals and plants
b. gymnastics
c. $25y + 32x = 51z$
d. $e = mc^2$
e. H_2O
f. the countries of the world
g. the 15th century
h. the Internet
i. vocabulary

48.2 Look at the subjects in A on page 98. Which are your favorite subjects? Which ones do you *not* like?

48.3 Look at the picture for 30 seconds. Then cover it. How many of the ten objects can you remember? Write them down in English.

48.4 Which of the things in B (on page 98) are in the room where you study English? Write down the words for everything you see.

48.5 Choose verbs from C (on page 98) to fill in the blanks below. Put the verbs in the correct form.

Carla did well in school. She always found it easy to (1) ..*learn*.., and she always (2) .... her homework. She (3) .... all her exams. Now she is in college, and she is (4) .... biology. She is also (5) .... a special chemistry course. Carla likes to sit in lectures, listen to the lecturer, and (6) .... notes. She will (7) .... her final exams next month. If she (8) ...., she will (9) .... a degree in biology. If she (10) ...., she will be very sad. She would like to become a biology teacher. She would like to (11) .... lectures.

UNIT 49 Communications

A Letters

Don't forget to put a **stamp** on the **envelope**.
Don't forget to **mail** the letters.

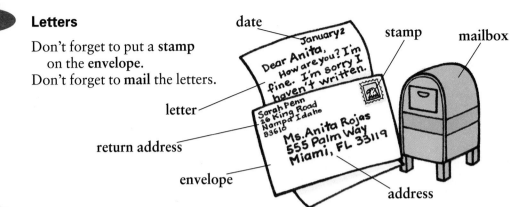

date

Dear Anita,
How are you? I'm fine. I'm sorry I haven't written.

January 2

stamp

mailbox

letter

Sarah Penn
26 King Road
Nampa, Idaho
83610

Ms. Anita Rojas
555 Palm Way
Miami, FL 33119

return address

envelope

address

B Telephone and fax

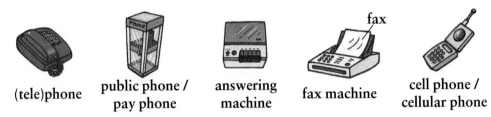

(tele)phone

public phone / pay phone

answering machine

fax machine

fax

cell phone / cellular phone

Juan **makes** a lot of **phone calls**. He **calls** his girlfriend every day.
Amporn **sent** me a **fax** yesterday. / Amporn **faxed** me yesterday.
What is your **phone number / fax number**?
It's 555-0718 [five-five-five, oh-seven-one-eight].

C A typical phone conversation

NICK: Hello?
SUE: Hi, Nick. This is Sue. Can I speak to Kim, please?
NICK: I'm sorry, but she just went out. Can I take a message?
SUE: Yeah, could you tell her I called? I'll call back later.
NICK: OK. I'll tell her.
SUE: Thanks. Bye.
NICK: Bye.

D E-mail

computer

monitor

keyboard

mouse

Anna gets a lot of **e-mail**.
What is your **e-mail address**?
It's mollflanders@cup.org [Moll Flanders at C-U-P dot org].

Tip: If possible, get an example of a letter and an e-mail in English. Write down any useful words or phrases in them.

Exercises

49.1   **Do you have any of the things on page 100? Make a list.**
answering machine

49.2   **What are the names of these things?**

1. ..*keyboard*..   4. ....   7. ....

2. ....   5. ....   8. ....

3. ....   6. ....   9. ....

49.3   **Complete this phone conversation.**

MARI: Hello?
JOHN: Hello, Mari. (1) .... is John. Can I (2) .... to Akira,
         please?
MARI: I'm (3) ...., but he's at work. Can I (4) .... a
         message?
JOHN: No, thanks. I'll (5) .... back later.
MARI: OK. Bye.
JOHN: Bye.

49.4   **Write down these numbers and addresses. Then read them aloud.**

1. Two telephone or fax numbers that are important to you.
2. Two e-mail addresses that are important to you.

49.5   **Answer these questions.**

1. Which is quickest – a phone call, a fax, an e-mail, or a letter?   *a phone call*
2. Which is cheapest – a phone call, a fax, an e-mail, or a letter?
3. Which of these have you sent – a letter, a fax, or an e-mail? Have you
   received all of them?
4. Which is your favorite way of communicating with a friend?
5. Which do you use most often for business communication?

UNIT 50 — On vacation

A Vacation (noun)

We **had a** wonderful **vacation** in Mexico last year.
I'm not working this week. **I'm on vacation**.
Are you **going on vacation** next summer?

B Types of vacations

We are going on **a package tour** to Hong Kong. [includes everything: flights, hotel, etc.]
We're going to take a **winter vacation** this year. [often means skiing / winter sports]
I want to **go camping** this year. [sleep in a tent]
A **bus tour** is a cheap way to go on vacation. [going with a group in a big bus]

C Transportation

We're going **by car / by train / by bus**. (See Units 14 and 41.)
Are you **flying** to Seattle from Vancouver?
No, we're going **by ferry**. [a ship where you can take your car with you]

D Don't forget to take . . .

your **passport** (if you are going to another country).
a **visa**. [a special stamp in your passport to go to some countries]
your **tickets**.
traveler's checks and some **currency**. [money of the country you're going to]
a **camera**.
a **phrase book** (if you don't speak the language).
your **luggage**. [suitcases, bags, etc.]

E When you are there . . .

send some **postcards**.
try the **local food**.
enjoy the **nightlife**. [discos, clubs, etc.]
go to the **Tourist Information Office/Center**
    if you have any questions.
have a good time! [Enjoy yourself!]

Exercises

50.1   Fill in the blanks with words from page 102.

1. A: Are you working on Monday?
   B: No, I'll be .... vacation next week.
2. A: Did you try the .... food while you were traveling?
   B: No, I just had hamburgers every day.
3. A: Did you have a good .... in Thailand?
   B: Yes, it was wonderful.
4. A: Are you flying to Italy?
   B: No, I'm going .... train.

50.2   These people are talking about their vacations. What type of vacation did they take?

1. Everything was included – meals, hotels, flights.
2. We were on the same bus for seven days. I was very tired.
3. It wasn't very good. There wasn't much snow.
4. We cooked our meals outdoors every day.

50.3   Choose the best answer.

1. Which is usually faster – a car or a ferry?
2. Which is usually cheaper – traveling by car or by plane?
3. Which can you take more luggage on – a ferry or a plane?
4. Which one often lets you see more as you travel – a car or a plane?

50.4   Write the names of these things you may need on a trip.

1. ..*currency*.......   3. ....   5. ....

2. ....   4. ....   6. ....

50.5   What do you call . . .

1. checks you can use in different countries? t................   c...........
2. a special stamp or paper for your passport to enter a country? a v...............
3. cards with pictures that you mail to friends and family? p...............
4. discos, clubs, and other entertainment at night? n...............

UNIT 51 Shopping

A Kinds of stores and shops

hardware store   supermarket   bookstore   bakery

gift shop

toy store

post office   pharmacy   hairdresser/hairstylist   newsstand

B Department store

A **department store** is a large store that sells different things (e.g., **clothes, furniture, stationery** [pens, paper, etc.], **cosmetics** [beauty products], etc.).

DIRECTORY	JD NICKELS	DIRECTORY
• **BASEMENT** food, sports equipment	• **SECOND FLOOR** women's fashions	• **FOURTH FLOOR** electronics, furniture
• **MAIN FLOOR** cosmetics, shoes stationery	• **THIRD FLOOR** children's clothes, toys, menswear	• **FIFTH FLOOR** garden restaurant

C Going shopping

A **salesclerk/salesperson** helps you find things and sells you things.

You pay for things at the **cashier / cash register**.

You get a **receipt**. [a piece of paper that shows what you bought and the price]

D Useful phrases

Can I help you?

How much does this **cost**?

Can I pay **by check / credit card**?
No, **cash** only.

Sorry, I only have a $100 **bill**; I don't have any **change**. [coins]

Can I **try it on**? [put on clothes to see how they look or fit]

Do you have **a bigger size / a smaller size / a different color**?

Would you like a **(shopping) bag**?

cash

coins/change

checkbook

credit card

Exercises

51.1 Match the item with the store.

| toy store hardware store bakery gift shop pharmacy newsstand |

1. aspirin

3. hammer

5. souvenir T-shirt

2. beach ball

4. magazine

6. bread

51.2 Where do you need to go?

1. I want to get a newspaper. *a newsstand*
2. My hair is too long.
3. I need some stamps.
4. We have to get Jim a present.
5. I'd like to buy a book.
6. I want to buy everything in one store.

51.3 Look at the department store directory in B on page 104. Which floor will you go to if you want to buy . . .

1. an armchair?
2. lipstick?
3. a cup of tea?
4. a package of tea?
5. a skirt?
6. some tennis balls?
7. a pair of boots?
8. some baby clothes?
9. a tie?
10. a TV?
11. pens?
12. a doll?

51.4 Write the words for these definitions.

1. a person who sells things in a store *salesclerk/salesperson*
2. money (not a check or credit card)
3. a person who cuts and styles hair
4. "plastic money"
5. a floor lower than the main floor
6. the place where you pay for things in a store
7. a piece of paper that you get when you buy something

51.5 Fill in the blanks in the conversation.

CUSTOMER: How much does this shirt (1) .... ?
SALESCLERK: $29.99.
CUSTOMER: OK, I'll take it. Can I (2) .... by credit card?
SALESCLERK: Of course. I'll put your receipt in the (3) ....

In a hotel

A   At the reception desk (the front desk)

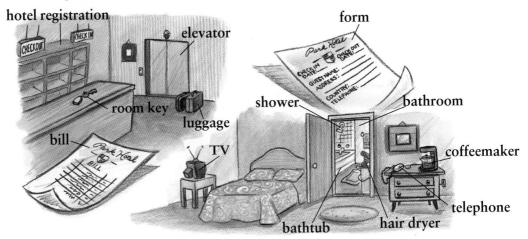

I'd like a **single room** [for one person] / a **double room** [for two people].
How much is a single room?
I'd like **a nonsmoking room**, if possible. [Smoking is not allowed.]
I have a **reservation**. [I booked/reserved a room in advance.] My name is . . .

The desk clerk may say:
   Your room is on the **ninth floor**. The **elevator** is over there.
   Here is your **key / room key**.
   Would you like some help with your **luggage**?
   Could you **fill out** this **form**, please?
   Sign here, please. [Write your name.]

When you leave, you say:
   I'm **checking out** now.
   Can I have the **bill**, please?

B   Using the telephone

How do I get an **outside line**? [You want to call someone outside the hotel.]
What is the **country code** for Taiwan/Brazil?
Can I have **room service**, please? [Someone brings food/drink to your room.]
Can I have a **wake-up call** at 6:30 a.m., please? [You want a telephone call to
   wake you up at 6:30 a.m.]

C   Changing money

You can often change money in a big hotel. Here are some useful phrases.
   Can I **change/exchange** some money, please?
   Can I **change** some dollars **into** yen, please? [yen = Japanese **currency**]
   How many yen **to the** dollar right now?
   Can I **cash** a traveler's check? [exchange a traveler's check for money]

Exercises

52.1 Look at the pictures and complete the conversation with words from page 106.

GUEST: Can I have a (1) ..double...... room for tonight, please?

DESK CLERK: Would you like a (2) .... room?

GUEST: Yes, please. And does the room have a (3) ....?

DESK CLERK: All our rooms have a TV, a (4) ...., and a

(5) .... I can give you Room 225. It's on the second

(6) .... Here is your (7) .... The

(8) .... is over there. Would you like some help with your

(9) ....?

GUEST: No, thanks. I have only one suitcase.

52.2 Match what you want with what you need. Draw lines.

You want:
1. to have coffee in your room
2. to go to the top floor
3. to unlock your door
4. to get up at 6 a.m.
5. to call someone in another country
6. to watch the news
7. to wash your hair
8. to dry your hair

You need:
a. the elevator
b. an outside line
c. a shower
d. a coffeemaker
e. a hair dryer
f. a wake-up call
g. a TV
h. a key

52.3 Do you know?

1. How much does a hotel room cost in the capital of your country?
2. What is the country code for the U.S. if you call from your country?
3. How many U.S. dollars are there to your own currency?
4. Why are traveler's checks useful when you are traveling?

52.4 Write six questions that you can ask in a hotel beginning with *Can I. . . .*
Can I have a wake-up call, please?

Eating out

A Places where you can eat

cafe: You can have coffee or tea and a **snack** there. [something small to eat like a sandwich or a piece of cake] They sometimes serve meals there too. Some cafes let you sit at your table for a long period of time.

restaurant: You go there for a full meal; often more expensive than a cafe.

coffee shop: A small restaurant that serves inexpensive meals, coffee/tea, etc.

deli: A store that sells cooked meats, cheese, salads, and sandwiches that you can take out to eat in a different place.

fast-food restaurant: You can get a quick hot meal there (e.g., a hamburger and french fries). (See Unit 43.)

B In a restaurant – the menu

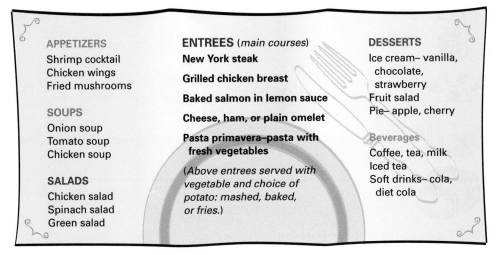

APPETIZERS
Shrimp cocktail
Chicken wings
Fried mushrooms

SOUPS
Onion soup
Tomato soup
Chicken soup

SALADS
Chicken salad
Spinach salad
Green salad

ENTREES (*main courses*)
New York steak
Grilled chicken breast
Baked salmon in lemon sauce
Cheese, ham, or plain omelet
Pasta primavera–pasta with fresh vegetables
(*Above entrees served with vegetable and choice of potato: mashed, baked, or fries.*)

DESSERTS
Ice cream– vanilla, chocolate, strawberry
Fruit salad
Pie– apple, cherry

Beverages
Coffee, tea, milk
Iced tea
Soft drinks– cola, diet cola

The **entree** is the main dish of the meal.

A **soft drink** (also called **soda** or **pop**) is a sweet-flavored drink without alcohol, e.g., cola.

C Ordering food

WAITRESS: Are you ready to order?

CUSTOMER: Yes, I'd like the shrimp cocktail, tomato soup, and steak.

WAITRESS: Mashed potatoes, baked potato, or fries?

CUSTOMER: Fries, please.

WAITRESS: How would you like your steak – rare, medium, or well-done?

CUSTOMER: Well-done, please.

WAITRESS: And what would you like to drink?

CUSTOMER: Coffee, please.

(*later*)

WAITRESS: Is everything all right?

CUSTOMER: Yes, everything's fine, thanks.

Exercises

53.1 Which of the places in A on page 108 would you go to if you . . .

1. want to buy a sandwich in the morning to eat at lunchtime at work? *a deli*
2. want a romantic dinner for two?
3. have three small children with you?
4. are meeting a friend who might be late?

53.2 Do you have all the places in A in your country? Write down all the places you have. Give an example of an eating place of this type.
fast-food restaurant – McDonald's

53.3 Look at the menu on page 108.

1. What would you eat from the menu?
2. What would a vegetarian eat? (Vegetarians don't eat meat.)
3. Can you find four dishes made with chicken?
4. Which one is a soft drink: coffee, milk, or cola?

53.4 Choose one of the words in the box that can go with each of the words in each group.

steak   omelet   potatoes   ice cream   soup   salad

1. You can have tomato/vegetable/chicken .....*soup*...... to start.
2. Would you like a cheese/ham/plain ....?
3. I'll have the chicken/spinach/fruit ....
4. I'd like the mashed / baked / french fried ....
5. Can I have the chocolate/strawberry/vanilla ...., please?
6. Do you like your .... well-done / medium / rare?

53.5 Correct the mistakes in this conversation.

WAITER: Are you ready ~~for~~ *to* order?
CUSTOMER: Yes. I like the vegetable soup and a hamburger, please.
WAITER: What would you like your hamburger? Rare, medium, or done good?
CUSTOMER: Medium.
WAITER: Anything to drink?
CUSTOMER: A iced tea, please.

53.6 Cover page 108 and write down all the words you can remember. Then look at the page again and write down any words you forgot.

Tip: Sometimes restaurants in other countries have English menus for tourists. Look at one of these. Write down any useful words you find.

Sports

A   Ball games

People **play** all these sports. I **play** golf. Do you **play** tennis?

| soccer | football | tennis | basketball |

| baseball | volleyball | golf | table tennis (Ping-Pong) |

B   Other popular sports

Use **go** with most of these sports (e.g., I **go** running. She **goes** skiing.)
But use **do** with judo and karate: He **does** judo. I **do** karate. (See Unit 4.)

| swimming | running | sailing | ice-skating |

| bowling | cycling | judo/karate | skiing |

C   Asking questions about sports

Do you play any sports? Yes, **I go** swimming/cycling/sailing/bowling.
Do you play soccer/football/tennis/volleyball?
What's your favorite sport? I like ice-skating **best**.

D   Where we play/do sports

You play tennis/volleyball/basketball on a **court**. You play golf on a **course**.
You play football/soccer/baseball on a **field**. You swim in a **swimming pool**.

Exercises

54.1 Cover page 110 and try to remember the names of these sports.

1. ...*cycling*......   3. ....   5. ....

2. ....   4. ....   6. ....

54.2 What sports do you think of when you see . . . ?

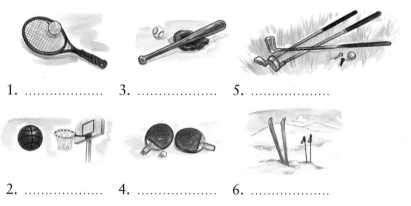

1. ....   3. ....   5. ....

2. ....   4. ....   6. ....

54.3 Ask questions for these answers.

1. Why do you ...*do karate / like karate*..?
   Because it's great exercise and it's good for self-defense.

2. ....?
   I like running best.

3. ....?
   No, I don't play any at all. I prefer watching TV.

4. Do you ....?
   Yes. I go to the swimming pool every Friday.

54.4 Write the names of sports you have played. Which ones do you like?
Which do you not like? Which ones would you like to try?

Tip: Make a page in your vocabulary book for "sports." Look at the sports
pages of an English-language newspaper. Write down the names of sports
you do not know. Look them up in a dictionary.

A   Types of movies

a western

a comedy

a science
fiction movie

an action movie

a musical

a cartoon /
an animated film

a horror movie

a crime /
detective movie

a love story /
a romantic movie

Do you like **westerns**?
   Not really; I like **comedies** best.
The best **science fiction movie** I've ever seen was *Star Wars*.
If I see a **horror movie**, I can't sleep.

B   People in movies

Zelda Glitzy is a **movie star**.
She lives in Hollywood.
She is **in** the new James Bond movie.
Sean Connery **played** James Bond in *Goldfinger*
   and other early James Bond movies.
I like movies by Italian **directors**.

C   Watching movies

Do you **go to the movies** often?
   Yes, I go all the time.
   No, I mostly **watch videos** at home.
What's at the movies this week?
   There's an animated film called *Pokémon*.
Have you **seen** *Star Wars*?
   Yes, I saw it **on TV**.
Did you like *Titanic*?
   Yes, I **loved it / enjoyed it**.
   No, it was **boring**. [makes you want to fall asleep]

Exercises

55.1   **What types of movies are these?**

1. Some cowboys rob a train.   *western*
2. A flying saucer lands from Mars.
3. A dead person comes back to life.
4. James Bond saves the world.
5. Mickey Mouse goes to the movies.
6. A man falls in love with his teacher.
7. A bank is robbed, and the bank robbers get away . . . or do they?
8. There is lots of singing and dancing.

55.2   **How many words for other types of movies can you make with the letters of ROMANTIC?**

```
          _ R I M _
          _ O _ _ _ R
      C _ M _ _ Y
          A _ T _ _ N
  S _ _ _ N C _ F _ _ _ _ _ N
      W _ _ T _ _ N
      M _ _ I C _ L
          C A _ _ O O _
```

55.3   **Fill in the blanks.**

1. Do you prefer to go .... movies or to watch TV?
2. We .... a video last night.
3. Who .... James Bond in *You Only Live Twice*?
4. Was Marlon Brando .... *The Godfather*?
5. A lot of big .... live in Hollywood.
6. Steven Spielberg is a famous movie ....

55.4   **Answer these questions about *yourself*.**

1. Name one science fiction movie you have seen.
2. Who is your favorite movie star?
3. Do you like detective movies? Can you name one?
4. Can you watch horror movies?

55.5   **Try to name one example of each type of movie from page 112!**

55.6   **Write down the English names of three movies you have seen recently. You can learn vocabulary by remembering the English names of movies.**

Leisure at home

A **TV, radio, music, video**

I **watch TV** every evening. (*not* I ~~see~~ TV.)
Did you **watch/see** the movie about John F. Kennedy?
I **listen to** the radio every morning. (*not* I ~~hear~~ the radio.)
What **programs** do you like best on TV and radio?
    I like **watching** movies on TV. (*or* I like to watch . . .)
I like **listening to** music on the radio. (*or* I like to listen . . .)
I often **listen to CDs** or **tapes** when I am relaxing.
On weekends, we usually **watch a video**.

B **Hobbies/activities at home**

A lot of kids / young people **play computer games**
    every day.
Do you use **the Internet**? / Are you **on the Internet**?
I really like **cooking**.
Do you like **gardening**?
We **grow flowers** and **vegetables** in our garden.
I live in an apartment. I don't have **a garden**, but I
    have a lot of **house plants**.

C **Reading**

I **read** a lot at home.
What do you read?
    I read **novels**. [long stories]
    I like **books about** nature / different countries.
    I like **magazines about** rock music, computers,
        and sports.
Do you read the **newspaper** every day?

D **Time with other people**

Sometimes we **invite friends over** / we **have friends over**.
    [We ask them to come to our home.]
I often **have people over** / **have friends over for dinner**.
My best friend **stays over** sometimes.
        [sleeps in my house/apartment]
I **talk to** my friends **on the phone** every evening.
    or I **call** my friends every evening.

E **Just relaxing**

Sometimes, I just **do nothing**.
I like to **take a nap** after lunch.
    [a short sleep, usually during the day]

Exercises

56.1 What are these people doing?

1. She's ....   4. She's ....

2. He's ....   5. She's ....

3. He's .... the ....   6. He's .... to ....

56.2 Fill in the missing verbs.

1. Sometimes I ...*listen*......... to CDs or tapes.
2. I .... to my sister on the phone every Sunday.
3. Some people like to .... a nap after lunch.
4. Do you ever .... friends over for dinner?
5. The children .... computer games every evening.
6. Do you want to .... a video tonight?
7. Did you .... the TV program about China yesterday?
8. My father .... vegetables in his garden.

56.3 Answer these questions about *yourself*.

1. If you have friends over, what do you like to do?
2. Does anyone stay over at your house/apartment?
3. What do you like to read most?
4. How often do you call your friends?

56.4 Interesting or boring? Put these leisure activities in order, from *most interesting* to *most boring*, in your opinion.

| gardening | cooking | reading | using the Internet |
| istening to music | | doing nothing | watching videos |

Crime

A **crime** is an action that is against the law. People who **commit** [do] serious crimes are called **criminals**.

A   Crimes, criminals, and verbs

Crime	Description	Criminal	Verb
robbery	steal from a person or a place (e.g., a bank)	a robber	to rob somebody; to rob a place (e.g., to rob a bank)
burglary	enter a place with force [**break in**] in order to steal	a burglar	to burglarize a place; to break into a home
theft	steal something (e.g., a car, jewels)	a thief (a car thief, a jewel thief)	to steal something
shoplifting	steal from a store while pretending to be a customer	a shoplifter	to shoplift; to steal things from a store

There was **a burglary** at the school during the night.
Burglars **broke into** the building after midnight.
There was a **robbery** at the bank this morning.
A robber **robs** a person or a place.
    That bank **was robbed** yesterday.
    My friend **was robbed** at the shopping mall.
A thief **steals** something.
    Somebody **stole** my bicycle. (*not* Somebody ~~robbed~~ my bicycle.)
I **was robbed** at the shopping mall yesterday. (*not* I was ~~stolen~~.)

B   The law

A student **was arrested for** shoplifting this morning.
The police came to the school and spoke to the principal.
The student has to **go to court** next week.
If she is **guilty**, she will have to **pay a fine**.
If she is **innocent**, she can go home.
I don't think she will **go to prison**.

C   Other crime problems

Some **vandals** broke the store windows.
    [people who break and damage things]
We have a lot of **vandalism** in my city.
Computer **hackers** illegally take or change information
    on someone else's computer. **Hacking** can be dangerous.
Speeding can lead to disaster. [driving a car faster than the
    legal speed limit]

Exercises

57.1 **What do you call . . .**

1. a person who steals cars?   *a car thief*
2. a person who walks into a bank and steals money?
3. a person who steals things from stores while pretending to be a shopper?
4. a person who breaks into people's houses and apartments to steal?
5. a person who steals jewels?

57.2 **Fill in the blanks.**

1. The police officer a*rrested*....... him for shoplifting.
2. Some v.................. destroyed all the flowers in the park.
3. The police stopped her for s.................. She was doing 80 mph where the speed limit was 55.
4. He had to pay a f.................. of $50 for parking his car in the wrong place.
5. The police made a mistake; she was i.................. She did not steal the money.
6. There are a lot of b.................. in this part of the city, so always close the windows and lock the door.
7. A computer h.................. was sent to prison for stealing credit card information on the Internet.

57.3 **What do you think should happen to these people? Choose from the list (a – i) on the right. If you do not like the choices in the list, what do you think should happen to them?**

1. A student with no money stole a book from a bookstore.
2. A man was driving 90 mph and crashed his car, killing two people.
3. A woman parked her car and blocked traffic.
4. A teenager broke some lights in the park.
5. A rich woman was caught shoplifting at a jewelry store.
6. Burglars broke into a home, stealing a TV, cash, and some watches.

a. fine of $100
b. 30 years in prison
c. six months in prison
d. the death penalty
e. must work in a hospital for six months
f. must not drive a car for a year
g. prison for life
h. five years in prison
i. must do **community service** [work in the community without pay]

57.4 **What do you think? Put all the crimes on page 116 in a list, from *least serious* to *most serious*.**

57.5 **Choose five or six words on page 116 and use them to make your own sentences.**

UNIT 58   The media

A   TV and radio programs

The news is on TV / on the radio at 6 o'clock every night. [a report about important things that have happened recently] (*not* The news ~~are~~ on TV.)

Do you watch **soap operas / soaps**? *Days of Our Lives* is my favorite. [Soap operas are continuing dramatic stories about a group of people.]

I like **nature programs** best. [programs about animals, birds, etc.]

I watched **a documentary** last night about immigration. [a program that gives information about a topic, based on facts]

On **talk shows**, famous people talk to a host about their lives.

The children watch **cartoons** on Saturday mornings. [programs with drawings that move.] (See Unit 55.)

I always watch **sports programs** and **movies** on TV.

B   Newspapers and magazines

In most countries there are **morning newspapers** and **afternoon** or **evening newspapers**.

Every week/month, I buy a **magazine**.

My mother buys **women's magazines**.

I like **news magazines** like *Newsweek* and *Time*.

My little brother buys **comics / comic books**. [magazines with stories told in pictures]

Other types of magazines: **sports magazines / computer magazines / teen magazines / fashion magazines** (See Unit 56.)

C   Media and technology

Do you have **satellite TV**?

How many **channels** do you get? We get 25.

You can read some newspapers **on the Internet**.

satellite dish   computer

D   People and the media

There was **an interview with** the President on TV last night.

Reporters are outside Zelda Glitzy's house. [people whose job is to discover information about news events and describe them for newspapers, TV, etc.]

My sister is **a journalist**; she writes for *The Valley* newspaper. [person who writes news stories and articles for newspapers, magazines, TV, etc.]

Exercises

58.1 **Fill in the blanks with words from page 118.**

1. The news ..*is*............ on Channel 3 at 9 o'clock every night.
2. There was a .... about air pollution on TV last night.
3. Some people read .... magazines to get ideas about clothing.
4. I saw a .... program about birds in Antarctica.
5. My sister is 14; she reads .... magazines every week. She likes the love stories.
6. With my computer I can get the sports news on the ....
7. Most young children don't read newspapers; they prefer to read ....

58.2 **Match the left-hand column with the right-hand column. Draw lines.**

1. a movie star talks about his family life   a. international news
2. movie about elephants in Africa   b. sports program
3. soccer cup final   c. soap opera
4. reports from all over the world   d. nature program
5. Maria decides to marry John (again)   e. talk show

58.3 **What can you find in these magazines? Match the left-hand column with the right-hand column. Draw lines.**

1. a computer magazine   a. articles about health, diet, family
2. a women's magazine   b. pictures of pop music stars
3. a news magazine   c. news about the Internet
4. a teen magazine   d. interviews with politicians

58.4 **What do you call . . .**

1. a person who discovers information and describes it for newspapers, TV, etc? *a reporter*
2. a person who writes articles in newspapers and magazines?
3. a newspaper you can buy every day after about 5 p.m.?
4. a magazine that children read, with cartoon pictures?
5. a TV program with factual information, sometimes analyzing problems in society?

58.5 **Answer these questions about *yourself*.**

1. Do you read a morning, afternoon, or evening newspaper?
2. How many TV channels do you get?
3. How many hours of TV do you watch every day?
4. What are your favorite kinds of TV programs? your favorite radio shows?

58.6 **Write a paragraph about the media in your country. Use words from page 118.**

Everyday problems

A At home

The TV **isn't working**. Can you **repair/fix** it?

The washing machine is **broken**. We need to **repair/fix** it.

The plants **are dying**.
    Did you forget to **water** them?

The room is **messy**. I have to **clean it up / clean up the room**.

I lost my keys. Will you help me **look for** them?

You **cut** your finger. You should
put on a Band-Aid.

You **had an argument with** a friend. Will you **apologize**?
    [say "I'm sorry."]

B At work

Carla had a bad day at work yesterday. First, she was
late for work.

She had **too much work to do**.
[more work than she could do]

Her co-worker was **in a bad mood**.
[felt angry or sad]

Her **computer crashed**.
[The computer stopped working.]

The photocopier was **out of order**.

The coffeemaker **wasn't working**.

Tip: When you need to make a list of things to do, make it in English, e.g.:
Fix my bike.   Water the plants.   Clean up my desk.

Exercises

59.1 Look at the pictures. What is the problem?

1. _The coffeemaker isn't working._ ....
2. ....
3. ....
4. ....
5. ....
6. ....
7. ....
8. ....

59.2 Write down three nouns that can go with these words.

1. broken _window/cup/glass_ ....
2. cut ....
3. messy ....
4. late for ....
5. a .... that isn't working
6. fix a ....

59.3 Which of these would be big problems for you? Which would be small problems?

1. a TV that doesn't work
2. dying plants
3. a cut finger
4. late for work
5. a co-worker in a bad mood
6. a photocopier that is out of order
7. a coffeemaker that isn't working
8. a broken washing machine
9. a messy bedroom
10. an argument with a friend
11. a computer crash
12. lost keys
13. too much work

59.4 Look at Carla's problems in B (page 120). What could she do?

She was late for work – leave home earlier next time.

59.5 Can you think of three everyday problems that you or people you know have had recently? Write them down in English. Use a dictionary if you need to.

Global problems

Natural disasters

There was a **hurricane / snowstorm / forest fire** last year.
hurricane [extremely strong winds that can cause great damage]
snowstorm [a storm with a lot of snow and strong winds at the same time]
forest fire [Trees catch fire and fire spreads quickly, often when it is very dry.]
California has had a lot of **earthquakes.** [The earth moves.]
The town was severely damaged by **floods** after the heavy rains. [Water covers
  an area that is usually dry.]

hurricane   snowstorm   forest fire

Problems caused by people

There are too many people in some places. Cities are too **crowded.**
Many people are . . .
  poor. [They do not have enough money.]
  hungry. [They do not have enough food.]
  homeless. [They do not have a place to live.]
  unemployed. [They do not have jobs.]

There is a lot of **pollution** in many cities. [The air, water, or earth is dirty and
  harmful to people, plants, and animals, especially because of chemicals or
  waste.]
The **air pollution** is very bad today.
The river is **polluted**, and a lot of fish have died.

Several countries are now at **war.** [fighting between two or more countries or
  nationalities]

The **traffic jams** [too many cars on the road, moving very slowly] in the city are
  terrible **during (the) rush hour** [times when everyone is going to work or
  coming home].

He had a **car crash** on the freeway. [a serious car accident; one or more cars hit
  something or hit each other]

There's a teachers' **strike** today. [They will not work because of a disagreement.]
The bus drivers are **on strike.**

Exercises

60.1 What problems can you see in the pictures?

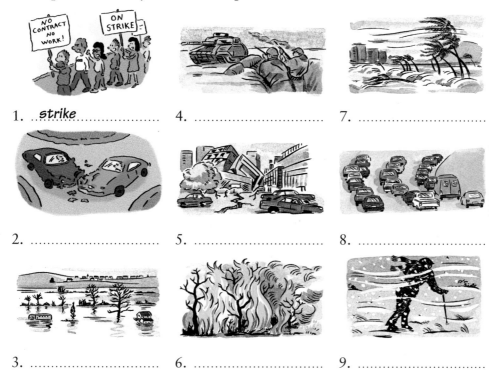

1. _strike_ 4. .... 7. ....

2. .... 5. .... 8. ....

3. .... 6. .... 9. ....

60.2 Write down the natural disasters in A (on page 122) and the names of some places where they have happened.

hurricane – Florida, Puerto Rico

60.3 Write down all the problems in B (on page 122) that you have in your country and the places where you have them.

poor people – small villages

60.4 Put all the words on page 122 into groups in any way that seems appropriate to you. Use as many groups as you wish.

hurricane, snowstorm, flood – problems because of the weather

60.5 Fill in the blanks with a word from page 122.

1. Cars make air .._pollution_........... worse in cities.
2. Their wages were very low, so the workers went on ....
3. My great-grandfather was a soldier in the First World ....
4. Sue had a car .... last year, but fortunately no one was hurt.
5. Japan often has ...., and Siberia often has ....
6. When people are .... they sometimes sleep on the streets.

Tip: Try to listen to or watch the news in English every day.

Common weights and measures

Linear Measures

1 foot = 12 inches
1 yard = 36 inches
1 mile = 5,280 feet

10 millimeters = 1 centimeter
100 centimeters = 1 meter
1000 meters = 1 kilometer

Weight/Mass

1 pound = 16 ounces
1 ton = 2,000 pounds

1000 milligrams = 1 gram
1000 grams = 1 kilogram
1000 kilograms = 1 metric ton

Liquid volume measures

1 tablespoon = 3 teaspoons
1 fluid ounce = 2 tablespoons
1 cup = 8 fluid ounces
1 pint = 16 fluid ounces = 2 cups
1 quart = 32 fluid ounces = 2 pints
1 gallon = 128 fluid ounces = 4 quarts
1 barrel = 31.5 gallons

10 milliliters = 1 centiliter
1000 milliliters = 1 liter

Time

1 minute = 60 seconds
1 hour = 60 minutes
1 day = 24 hours
1 year = 365 days

Temperature

0 degrees C / 32 degrees F   Freezing point of water
37 degrees C / 98.6 degrees F   Normal human body temperature
100 degrees C / 212 degrees F   Boiling point of water

List of irregular verbs

B

be (am/is/are)	was/were	been
beat	beat	beaten
become	became	become
begin	began	begun
bend	bent	bent
bet	bet	bet
bite	bit	bitten
blow	blew	blown
break	broke	broken
bring	brought	brought
build	built	built
burst	burst	burst
buy	bought	bought

C

catch	caught	caught
choose	chose	chosen
come	came	come
cost	cost	cost
cut	cut	cut

D

dig	dug	dug
do	did	done
draw	drew	drawn
drink	drank	drunk
drive	drove	driven

E

eat	ate	eaten

F

fall	fell	fallen
feed	fed	fed
feel	felt	felt
fight	fought	fought
find	found	found
fit	fit	fit
fly	flew	flown
forget	forgot	forgotten
freeze	froze	frozen

G

get	got	gotten
give	gave	given
go	went	gone
grow	grew	grown

H

hang	hung	hung
have	had	had
hear	heard	heard
hide	hid	hidden
hit	hit	hit
hold	held	held
hurt	hurt	hurt

K

keep	kept	kept
know	knew	known

L

lead	led	led
leave	left	left
lend	lent	lent
let	let	let
lose	lost	lost

M

make	made	made
mean	meant	meant
meet	met	met

P

pay	paid	paid
put	put	put

Q

quit	quit	quit

R

read	read	read
ride	rode	ridden
ring	rang	rung
rise	rose	risen
run	ran	run

S

say	said	said
see	saw	seen
sell	sold	sold
send	sent	sent
shake	shook	shaken
shine	shone	shone
shoot	shot	shot
show	showed	shown
shut	shut	shut
sing	sang	sung
sink	sank	sunk
sit	sat	sat
sleep	slept	slept
speak	spoke	spoken
spend	spent	spent
spread	spread	spread
stand	stood	stood
steal	stole	stolen
sweep	swept	swept
swim	swam	swum

T

take	took	taken
teach	taught	taught
tear	tore	torn
tell	told	told
think	thought	thought
throw	threw	thrown

U

understand	understood	understood

W

wake	woke	woken
wear	wore	worn
win	won	won
write	wrote	written

Phonetic symbols

Vowel sounds

Symbol	Examples	Symbol	Examples
/ɑ/	hot, father, sock, star	/ɔ/	saw, thought, ball
/æ/	hat, last, bag	/ɔɪ/	boy, join
/ɑɪ/	bite, ride, sky, height	/oʊ/	go, boat, below
/ɑʊ/	house, now	/ʊ/	put, good
/e/	let, head, said; *before* /r/: fair, rare	/u/	food, blue, shoe, lose
		/ʌ/	*stressed:* sun, love, under
/eɪ/	late, name, say	/ə/	*unstressed:* alone, label, collect, under
/i/	sleep, me, happy		
/ɪ/	fit, pin, if	/ɜ/	*before* /r/: bird, turn, earn

Consonant sounds

Symbol	Examples	Symbol	Examples
/b/	bid, rob	/s/	see, mouse, recent
/d/	did, under	/ʃ/	shoe, cash, nation
/ð/	this, mother, breathe	/t/	team, meet, matter, sent
/dʒ/	judge gentle	/tʃ/	church, rich, catch
/f/	foot, safe, laugh	/θ/	think, both
/g/	go, rug, bigger	/v/	visit, save
/h/	house, behind, whole	/w/	watch, away, wear; which, where–*Many North American speakers pronounce* /w/ *in such words and many pronounce* /hw/.
/j/	yes, useful, music		
/k/	kick, cook, quick		
/l/	look, ball, feel, pool		
/m/	many, some, damp		
/n/	none, sunny, sent	/z/	zoo, has, these
/ŋ/	ring, think, longer	/ʒ/	measure, beige, Asia
/p/	peel, soap, pepper		
/r/	read, carry, far, card–*In some parts of North America* /r/ *is not always pronounced at the ends of words or before consonants.*		

Index

bring back /'brɪŋ 'bæk/ 9
British /'brɪt·ɪʃ/ 36
broken /'broʊ·kən/ 59
broken arm /'broʊ·kən arm/ 3
brother /'brʌð·ər/ 3, 29
brown /braʊn/ 32
brush your teeth /brʌʃ jʊr tiθ/ 45
bulletin board /'bʊl·ə·tən bɔrd/ 48
burglar /'bɜr·glər/ 57
burglarize /'bɜr·glə,raɪz/ 57
burglary /'bɜr·glə·ri/ 57
bus /bʌs/ 4, 41
bus stop /bʌs stap/ 38
but /bʌt/ 15
butter /'bʌt·ər/ 21
buy /baɪ/ 20, 38
by bus /baɪ bʌs/ 4, 12, 50
by car /baɪ kar/ 4, 12, 50
by ferry /baɪ 'fer·i/ 50
by train /baɪ treɪn/ 1, 12, 50
bye /baɪ/ 49

cabin /'kæb·ən/ 39
cabinet /'kæb·ə·nət/ 44
cafe /kæ'feɪ/ 53
cake /keɪk/ 43
calf /kæf/ 40
call (v.) /kɔl/ 28, 33, 49, 56
call a friend /kɔl ə frend/ 12
camera /'kæm·rə/ 50
can I /kæn aɪ/ 38
can I help you /kæn aɪ help ju/ 51
can I speak to /kæn aɪ spik tu/ 49
can I take a message /kæn aɪ teɪk ə 'mes·ɪdʒ/ 49
can opener /kæn 'oʊ·pə·nər/ 26
can you tell me /kæn ju tel mi/ 13
Canada /'kæ·nə·də/ 36
Canadian /kə'neɪd·i·ən/ 36
cancer /'kæn·sər/ 33
capital letter /'kæp·ət·əl 'let·ər/ 1
car /kar/ 2, 26, 41
car crash /kar kræʃ/ 60
carpet /'kar·pət/ 46
carrot /'kær·ət/ 43
carry /'kær·i/ 14, 31
cartoon /kar'tun/ 55, 58
cash (n.) /kæʃ/ 51
cash (v.) /kæʃ/ 52
cash register /kæʃ 'redʒ·ə·stər/ 51
cashier /kæ'ʃɪr/ 51
cassette /kə'set/ 48
cat /kæt/ 40
catch /kætʃ/ 20
catch the bus/train/plane /kætʃ ðə bʌs/treɪn/pleɪn/ 14
caution /'kɔ·ʃən/ 42
CD /'si 'di/ 56
CD player /'si 'di 'pleɪ·ər/ 46

cell phone /'sel·foʊn/ 49
cellular phone /'sel·jə·lər 'foʊn/ 49
Celsius /'sel·si·əs/ 37
century /'sen·tʃə·ri/ 16
chair /tʃer/ 2, 30, 46
chalk /tʃɔk/ 48
chalkboard /'tʃɔk·bɔrd/ 48
change (n.) /tʃeɪndʒ/ 51
change (v.) /tʃeɪndʒ/ 41, 52
change into /tʃeɪndʒ 'ɪn·tu/ 52
change money /tʃeɪndʒ 'mʌn·i/ 38
channel /'tʃæn·əl/ 58
check /tʃek/ 51
check in /'tʃek 'ɪn/ 41
check out /'tʃek 'aʊt/ 52
check your luggage /'tʃek jʊr 'lʌg·ɪdʒ/ 41
checkbook /'tʃek·bʊk/ 51
cheese /tʃiz/ 53
chemical /'kem·ɪ·kəl/ 60
chemistry /'kem·ə·stri/ 48
cherry /'tʃer·i/ 53
chest /tʃest/ 30
chest of drawers /tʃest ʌv drɔrz/ 45
chick /tʃɪk/ 40
chicken /'tʃɪk·ən/ 40, 53
chicken breast /'tʃɪk·ən brest/ 53
chicken wings /'tʃɪk·ən wɪŋz/ 53
childish /'tʃaɪl·dɪʃ/ 23
Chile /'tʃɪl·i/ 36
Chilean /tʃɪ·'leɪ·ən/ 36
China /'tʃaɪ·nə/ 36
Chinese /,tʃaɪ 'niz/ 36
chocolate /'tʃak·lət/ 53
cholera /'kal·ə·rə/ 33
choose /tʃuz/ 20
chopsticks /'tʃap·stɪks/ 44
city /'sɪt·i/ 38, 39
city hall /'sɪt·i hɔl/ 38
class /klæs/ 3
clean the house /klin ðə haʊs/ 12
clean up /klin ʌp/ 59
climb /klaɪm/ 14
clock /klak/ 30
close (v.) /kloʊz/ 46
closed /kloʊzd/ 42
closet /'klaz·ət/ 45
clothes /kloʊðz/ 2, 31, 51
cloud /klaʊd/ 37
cloudy /'klaʊd·i/ 37
club /klʌb/ 50
coat /koʊt/ 31
coffee /'kɔ·fi/ 21,43, 53
coffee maker /'kɔ·fi 'meɪ·kər/ 44, 52, 59
coffee shop /'kɔ·fi ʃap/ 53
coffee table /'kɔ·fi 'teɪ·bəl/ 46
coin /kɔɪn/ 51
cola /'koʊ·lə/ 53

cold (adj.) /koʊld/ 10, 21, 34. 37
cold (n.) /koʊld/ 3, 33
college /'kal·ɪdʒ/ 47, 48
collocation /,ka·lə 'keɪ·ʃən/ 2
Colombia /kə 'lʌm·bi·ə/ 36
color /'kʌl·ər/ 32,46, 51
comb /koʊm/ 45
come /kʌm/ 6, 20
come across /,kʌm ə'krɔs/ 6
come back /,kʌm 'bæk/ 6
come back from /,kʌm 'bæk frʌm/ 6
come from /'kʌm 'frʌm/ 6
come home /'kʌm 'hoʊm/ 6, 12
come in /'kʌm 'ɪn/ 6
come on /'kʌm 'ɔn/ 6, 11
come out /'kʌm 'aʊt/ 6
come over /,kʌm 'oʊ·vər/ 6
come up /,kʌm 'ʌp/ 6, 11
comedy /'kam·əd·i/ 55
comes into /kʌmz 'ɪn·tu/ 6
comes out of /kʌmz 'aʊt ʌv/ 6
comfortable /'kʌm·fərt·ə·bəl/ 25
comic book /'kam·ɪk ,bʊk/ 58
comics /'kam·ɪks/ 58
commit /kə'mɪt/ 57
communication /kə,mju·nə'keɪ·ʃən/ 49
community service /kə'mju·nət·i 'sɜr·vəs/ 57
complete /kəm'plit/ 1
computer /kəm'pjut·ər/ 48, 49, 56, 58, 59
computer game /kəm'pjut·ər geɪm/ 56
computer science /kəm'pjut·ər 'saɪ·əns/ 48
congratulations /kən,græt·ʃ·ə'leɪ·ʃənz/ 13,
conjunction /kən'dʒʌŋ·ʃən/ 15
conservation /,kan·sər'veɪ·ʃən/ 39
continent /'kant·ən·ənt/ 36
convenient /kən'vin·jənt/ 25
cooking /'kʊk·ɪŋ/ 44, 56
cool /kul/ 2,3
correct (adj.) /kə'rekt/ 1, 25
correct (v.) /kə'rekt/ 1
cosmetic /kaz'met·ɪk/ 51
cost /kɔst/ 20
couch /kaʊtʃ/ 46
could you tell her I called? /kʊd ju tel hɜr aɪ kɔld/ 49
countable /'kaʊnt·ə·bəl/ 21
counter /'kaʊnt·ər/ 44
country /'kʌn·tri/ 36, 39
country code /'kʌn·tri koʊd/ 52
countryside /'kʌn·tri·saɪd/ 39
course /kɔrs/ 8, 48, 54
court /kɔrt/ 54, 57
cousin /'kʌz·ən/ 29
cow /kaʊ/ 40
co-worker /'koʊ,wɜr·kər/ 59

crash (v.) /kræʃ/ 59
crayon /'kreɪ·ən/ 48
credit card /'kred·ət kɑrd/ 51
crime /kraɪm/ 57
crime movie /kraɪm 'mu·vi/ 55
criminal /'krɪm·ən·əl/ 57
crowded /'kraʊd·əd/ 60
Cuba /'kju·bə/ 36
Cuban /'kju·bən/ 36
cup /kʌp/ 2, 21,44, 51
cup of coffee /kʌp ʌv 'kɔ·fi/
cup of tea /kʌp ʌv ti/ 3
cupboard /'kʌb·ərd/ 44
currency /'kɜr·ən·si/ 50
curtains /'kɜrt·ənz/ 46
customer /'kʌs·tə·mər/ 57
customs /'kʌs·təmz/ 41
cut /kʌt/ 20, 59
cycling /'saɪ·klɪŋ/ 33, 54

dance /dæns/ 5, 14
Danish /'deɪ·nɪʃ/ 36
dark /dɑrk/ 10, 32
date /deɪt/ 3, 49
daughter /'dɔt·ər/ 29
day /deɪ/ 16
day after tomorrow /deɪ 'æf·tər
tə'mɑr·oʊ/ 16
day before yesterday /deɪ bɪ'fɔr
'jes·tər·deɪ/ 16
dead /ded/ 28
death /deθ/ 28
death penalty /deθ 'pen·əl·ti/ 57
December /dɪ'sem·bər/ 6
decide /dɪ'saɪd/ 6
degree /dɪ'gri/ 37
deli /'del·i/ 53
dentist /'dent·əst/ 6, 33
depart /dɪ'pɑrt/ 11, 41
department store /dɪ'pɑrt·mənt
stɔr/ 38, 51
desk /desk/ 2, 48
desk clerk /desk klɜrk/ 52
dessert /dɪ'zɜrt/ 43, 52
detective movie /dɪ'tek·tɪv
'mu·vi/ 55
diagram /'daɪ·ə,græm/ 2
die /daɪ/ 28, 59
die of /daɪ ʌv/ 28
diet /'daɪ·ət/ 33
diet cola /'daɪ·ət 'koʊ·lə/ 53
different /'dɪf·rənt/ 51
difficult /'dɪf·ə·kəlt/ 23
difficulty /'dɪf·ə·kəl·ti/ 19
dig /dɪg/ 20
dining car /daɪn·ɪŋ kɑr/ 41
dinner /'dɪn·ər/ 3
director /də'rek·tər/ 55
discos /'dɪs·koʊz/ 50
disease /dɪ'ziz/ 33
disgusting /dɪs'gʌs·tɪŋ/ 22
dish /dɪʃ/ 44
dishtowel /'dɪʃ,taʊ·əl/ 44

dishwasher /'dɪʃ'wɑʃ·ər/ 44
dishwashing liquid /'dɪʃ'wɑʃ·ɪŋ
'lɪk·wəd/ 44
dislike /dɪs'laɪk/ 34
divorce /dɪ'vɔrs/ 28
divorced /dɪ'vɔrsd/ 28
do /du/ 5, 20
do a good job /du ə gʊd dʒɑb/ 5
do an exercise /du æn
'ek·sər,saɪz/ 2
do business with /du 'bɪz·nəs
wɪð/ 5
do exercises /du 'ek·sər,saɪz·əz/
5
do homework /du 'hoʊm·wɜrk/ 1,
48
do my homework /du maɪ
'hoʊm·wɜrk/ 6
do nothing /du 'nʌθ·ɪŋ/ 56
do the cooking /du ðə 'kʊk·ɪŋ/ 5
do the dishes /du ðə dɪʃ·ɪz/ 5, 6
do the housework /du ðə
'haʊs·wɜrk/ 5
do the laundry /du ðə 'lɔn·dri/ 5,
12
doctor /'dɑk·tər/ 5, 6, 33, 47
documentary /,dɑk·jə'ment·ə·ri/
58
dog /dɔg/ 40
doll /dɑl/ 51
door /dɔr/ 2
double room /'dʌb·əl rum/ 52
downtown /'daʊn'taʊn/ 4, 38
draw /drɔ/ 2
dreadful /'dred·fəl/ 22
dress /dres/ 2, 31
dresser /'dres·ər/ 45
drink (n.) /drɪŋk/ 2, 3, 21, 25,
43
drink (v.) /drɪŋk/ 20, 44
drinking water /'drɪŋ·kɪŋ 'wɔt·ər/
33
drive /draɪv/ 20
drive a bus /draɪv ə 'bʌs/ 14
drive a car /draɪv ə 'kɑr/ 14
drive a taxi /draɪv ə 'tæk·si/ 14
drive a truck /draɪv ə 'trʌk/ 14
driving test /'draɪ·vɪŋ test/ 8
dry /draɪ/ 2, 37
during /'dʊr·ɪŋ/ 60
Dutch /dʌtʃ/ 36

ear /ɪr/ 30
earth /ɜrθ/ 60
easily /'i·zə·li/ 19
easygoing /'i·zi,goʊ·ɪŋ/ 23
eat /it/ 2, 20, 44
eat out /it aʊt/ 52
economics /,i·kə'nɑm·ɪks/ 26
education /,edʒ·ə'keɪ·ʃən/ 2
egg /eg/ 40
Egypt /'i·dʒɪpt/ 36
Egyptian /,ɪ'dʒɪp·ʃən/ 36

elderly /'el·dər·li/ 32
electrical outlet /ɪ'lek·trɪ·kəl
'aʊt·lət/ 46
electronics /ɪ,lek'trɑn·ɪks/ 51
elementary school /,el·ə'men·tri
skul/ 48
elephant /'el·ə·fənt/ 40
elevator /'el·ə,veɪt·ər/ 52
e-mail /'i·meɪl/ 13, 49
e-mail address /'i·meɪl 'æd·res/
49
end /end/ 18
end table /end 'teɪ·bəl/ 46
endless /'en·dləs/ 26
engineer /,en·dʒə'nɪr/ 5
England /'ɪŋ·lənd/ 36
English /'ɪŋ·glɪʃ/ 36, 48
enjoy /ɪn'dʒɔɪ/ 55
entrance /'en·trəns/ 42
entree /'ɑn·treɪ/ 53
envelope /'en·və,loʊp/ 49
eraser /ɪ'reɪ·sər/ 48
essay /'es·eɪ/ 5
even /'i·vən/ 15
evening /'iv·nɪŋ/ 16, 27,58
every day /'ev·ri deɪ/ 35
everyday /'ev·ri,deɪ/ 12, 14, 21,
33, 43, 59
everywhere /'ev·ri,wer/ 18
exam /ɪg'zæm/ 2, 3, 8
example /ɪg'zæm·pəl/ 1
ex-boss /,eks'bɔs/ 25
ex-boyfriend /,eks'bɔɪ·frend/ 25
excellent /'ek·sə·lənt/ 22
exchange /ɪks'tʃeɪndʒ/ 52
excuse me /ɪk'skjuz mi/ 25, 38
exercise /'ek·sər,saɪz/ 33
ex-husband /,eks'hʌz·bənd/ 25
exit /'ek·sət/ 42
expect /ɪk'spekt/ 27
expensive /ɪk'spen·sɪv/ 24
ex-wife /,eks'waɪf/ 25
eye /aɪ/ 30, 32

fabulous /'fæb·jə·ləs/ 22
face /feɪs/ 30, 32
factory /'fæk·tə·ri/ 47
Fahrenheit /'fær·ən,haɪt/ 37
fail your exam /feɪl jʊr ɪg'zæm/
48
fair /fer/ 32
fall /fɔl/ 14, 16, 20, 27
fall asleep /fɔl ə'slip/ 45
family /'fæm·ə·li/ 29
family tree /'fæm·ə·li 'tri/ 29
fare /fer/ 41
farm /fɑrm/ 39, 40
farmer /'fɑr·mər/ 39, 47
farmland /'fɑrm·lænd/ 39
fashion /'fæʃ·ən/ 51, 58
fast /fæst/ 19, 26
fast food /fæst fud/ 43

karate /kəˈrɑt·i/ 54
keep /kip/ 20
Keep off the grass /kip ɔf ðə græs/ 42
key /ki/ 52
keyboard /ˈki·bɔrd/ 49
kill /kɪl/ 33
kilo /ˈki·loʊ/ 32
kind /kaɪnd/ 23
kind of /kaɪnd ʌv/ 23
kind to /kaɪnd tu/ 23
kitchen /ˈkɪtʃ·ən/ 44
knee /ni/ 30
knife /naɪf/ 2, 44
know /noʊ/ 20
Korean /kʌˈri·ən/ 36

ladies /ˈleɪd·iz/ 42
lake /leɪk/ 39
lamb /læm/ 40
land /lænd/ 2, 41
language /ˈlæŋ·ɡwɪdʒ/ 1, 36, 48
last /læst/ 17
late for /leɪt fɔr/ 59
lawyer /ˈlɔɪ·ər/ 47
learn /lɜrn/ 2, 48
leather /ˈleð·ər/ 40
leave /liv/ 20, 41
left /left/ 18
leg /leɡ/ 30
legal /ˈli·ɡəl/ 57
leisure /ˈli·ʒər/ 56
lend /lend/ 27
lesson /ˈles·ən/ 5
let /let/ 20
letter /ˈlet·ər/ 13, 49
librarian /laɪˈbrer·i·ən/ 38
library /ˈlaɪˌbrer·i/ 38
lift /lɪft/ 41
light (adj.) /laɪt/ 10, 32
light (n.) /laɪt/ 2, 46
light switch /laɪt swɪtʃ/ 46
lightning /ˈlaɪt·nɪŋ/ 37
like /laɪk/ 15, 34, 54
linguini /lɪŋˈwi·ni/ 43
lion /ˈlaɪ·ən/ 40
lip /lɪp/ 30
lipstick /ˈlɪp·stɪk/ 51
listen to /ˈlɪs·ən tu/ 5, 24, 56
listen to music /ˈlɪs·ən tu ˈmju·zɪk/ 46
listen to the radio /ˈlɪs·ən tu ðə ˈreɪd·i·oʊ/ 12, 45
living room /lɪv·ɪŋ rum/ 46
local food /ˈloʊ·kəl fud/ 50
long /lɔŋ/ 32
look at /lʊk æt/ 24
look for /lʊk fɔr/ 24, 38, 59
look forward to /lʊk ˈfɔr·wərd tu/ 24
look up /lʊk ʌp/ 24
loose /lus/ 27
lose /luz/ 20, 27, 59

loud /laʊd/ 19
loudly /ˈlaʊd·li/ 19
love /lʌv/ 34, 55
love story /lʌv ˈstɔr·i/ 55
luggage /ˈlʌɡ·ɪdʒ/ 14, 21, 41, 50, 52
lunch /lʌntʃ/ 3

macaroni /ˌmæk·əˈroʊ·ni/ 43
magazine /ˌmæɡ·əˈzin/ 51, 56, 58
mail (v.) /meɪl/ 49
mail a letter /meɪl ə ˈlet·ər/ 38
mailbox /ˈmeɪl·bɑks/ 49
main course /meɪn kɔrs/ 53
main floor /meɪn flɔr/ 51
make /meɪk/ 6, 20
make a decision /meɪk ə dɪˈsɪʒ·ən/ 6
make a meal /meɪk ə mil/ 6
make a mistake /meɪk ə məˈsteɪk/ 1, 2, 6
make a movie /meɪk ə ˈmu·vi/ 6
make a phone call /meɪk ə foʊn kɔl/ 6, 49
make a photocopy /meɪk ə ˈfoʊt·əˌkɑp·i/ 6
make a video /meɪk ə ˈvɪd·i·oʊ/ 6
make an appointment /meɪk æn əˈpɔɪnt·mənt/ 6
make breakfast /meɪk ˈbrek·fəst/ 6
make coffee /meɪk ˈkɔ·fi/ 6
make dinner /meɪk ˈdɪn·ər/ 6, 12
make lunch /meɪk lʌntʃ/ 6
make me feel angry /meɪk mi fil ˈæŋ·ɡri/ 6
make me feel nervous /meɪk mi fil ˈnɜr·vəs/ 6
make me feel sad /meɪk mi fil sæd/ 6
make tea/soup /meɪk ti/sup/ 6
malaria /məˈler·i·ə/ 33
man /mæn/ 2
manner /ˈmæn·ər/ 19
map /mæp/ 41
March /mɑrtʃ/ 16
marriage /ˈmær·ɪdʒ/ 28
married /ˈmær·id/ 28
mashed /mæʃt/ 53
match /mætʃ/ 1
math /ˌmæθ/ 48
mathematics /ˌmæθ·əˈmæt·ɪks/ 48
May /meɪ/ 16
meal /mil/ 3
meat /mit/ 40, 43
mechanic /məˈkæn·ɪk/ 47
media /ˈmid·i·ə/ 58
medicine cabinet/chest /ˈmed·ə·sən ˈkæb·ə·nət tʃest/ 45
medium /ˈmid·i·əm/ 53

medium height /ˈmid·i·əm haɪt/ 32
meet /mit/ 4, 5, 20
meeting /mit·ɪŋ/ 3, 5
men /mæn/ 42
menswear /ˈmenz·wer/ 51
messy /ˈmes·i/ 59
meter /ˈmit·ər/ 32
Mexican /ˈmeks·ɪ·kən/ 36
Mexico /ˈmeks·ɪ·koʊ/ 36
microwave /ˈmaɪ·krə·weɪv/ 44
middle /ˈmɪd·əl/ 18
middle-aged /ˌmɪd·əlˈeɪdʒd/ 32
milk /mɪlk/ 2, 21, 40, 43, 53
mineral water /ˈmɪn·ə·rəl ˈwɔt·ər/ 43
minus /ˈmaɪ·nəs/ 37
minute /ˈmɪn·ət/ 16
mirror /ˈmɪr·ər/ 45
misbehave /ˌmɪs·bɪˈheɪv/ 25
miss /mɪs/ 27
miss the bus /mɪs ðə bʌs/ 14
miss the plane /mɪs ðə pleɪn/ 14
miss the train /mɪs ðə treɪn/ 14
misspelled /mɪsˈspeld/ 25
mistake /məˈsteɪk/ 1
misunderstood /mɪsˌʌn·dərˈstʊd/ 25
modern /ˈmɑd·ərn/ 21
Monday /ˈmʌn·deɪ/ 16
money /ˈmʌn·i/ 21
monitor /ˈmɑn·ət·ər/ 49
monkey /ˈmʌŋ·ki/ 40
month /mʌnθ/ 16, 17
morning /ˈmɔr·nɪŋ/ 16, 45, 58
mosquito /məˈskit·oʊ/ 33
mother /ˈmʌð·ər/ 29
motorcycle /ˈmoʊt·ərˌsaɪ·kəl/ 41
mountain /ˈmaʊnt·ən/ 30, 39
mouse /maʊs/ 49
mouth /maʊθ/ 30
movie /ˈmu·vi/ 55, 58
movie star /ˈmu·vi stɑr/ 55
mug /mʌɡ/ 2, 44
museum /mjʊˈzi·əm/ 38
mushroom /ˈmʌʃ·rum/ 43, 53
music /ˈmju·zɪk/ 5, 48, 56
musical /ˈmju·zɪ·kəl/ 55
must /mʌst/ 3
mustache /ˈmʌs·tæʃ/ 32
my /maɪ/ 30

name /neɪm/ 28
nasty /ˈnæs·ti/ 23
nation /ˈneɪ·ʃən/ 39
natural /ˈnætʃ·ə·rəl/ 39
natural disasters /ˈnætʃ·ə·rəl dɪˈzæs·tər/ 60
nature /ˈneɪ·tʃər/ 39, 56, 58
near /nɪr/ 46
neck /nek/ 30
needle /ˈnid·əl/ 30
negative /ˈneɡ·ət·ɪv/ 23

nephew /'nef·ju/ 29
nerves /nɜrvz/ 25
never /'nev·ər/ 14, 16
news /nuz/ 21, 58
newspaper /'nuz·peɪ·pər/ 10, 12, 38, 56, 58
newsstand /'nuz·stænd/ 51
next /nekst/ 17, 46
nice /naɪs/ 22, 23
niece /nis/ 29
night /naɪt/ 27
nightgown /'naɪt·gaʊn/ 45
nightlife /'naɪt·laɪf/ 50
nightstand /'naɪt·stænd/ 45
night table /naɪt 'teɪ·bəl/ 45
nighttime /'naɪt,taɪm/ 45
no entry /noʊ 'en·tri/ 38
no parking /'noʊ 'par·kɪŋ/ 38
nonalcoholic /,nan·æl·kə'hɔ·lɪk/ 25
nonresident /,nan'rez·ə·dənt/ 25
nonsmoking /nan'smoʊ·kɪŋ/ 25, 52
noon /nun/ 16
normally /'nɔr·mə·li/ 12
nose /noʊz/ 30
not often /nat 'ɔ·fən/ 17
notebook /'noʊt·bʊk/ 2, 48
notice /'noʊt·əs/ 42
noun /naʊn/ 1
novel /'nav·əl/ 56
November /noʊ'vem·bər/ 16
now /naʊ/ 17
now and then /naʊ ænd ðen/ 17
nurse /nɜrs/ 47
nursing home /nɜrs·ɪŋ hoʊm/ 32

o'clock /ə'klak/ 17
occasionally /ə'keɪ·ʒən·əl·i/ 17
October /ak'toʊ·bər/ 16
of /ʌv/ 28
office /'ɔ·fəs/ 47
office building /'ɔ·fəs 'bɪl·dɪŋ/ 38
often /'ɔ·fən/ 17
old /oʊld/ 32
older /'oʊl·dər/ 32
on /ɔn/ 16, 28
on foot /ɔn fʊt/ 2, 12
on strike /ɔn straɪk/ 60
on the Internet /ɔn ðə 'ɪnt·ər,net/ 56
on the left /ɔn ðə left/ 18
on the phone /ɔn ðə foʊn/ 56
on the radio /ɔn ðə 'reɪd·i,oʊ/ 58
on the right /ɔn ðə raɪt/ 18
on the weekend /ɔn ðə 'wi·kend/ 16
on TV /ɔn ,ti·'vi/ 55, 58
on vacation /ɔn veɪ'keɪ·ʃən/ 50
once a week /wʌns ə wik/ 17
once a year /wʌns ə jɪr/ 14
one-way /,wʌn'weɪ/ 41
onion /'ʌn·jən/ 43, 53

only /'oʊn·li/ 15
open /'oʊ·pən/ 20
orange /'ar·əndʒ/ 43
out /aʊt/ 18
out of order /'aʊt ʌv 'ɔrd·ər/ 42, 59
out of town /'aʊt ʌv taʊn/ 18
outside line /'aʊt'saɪd laɪn/ 52
oven /'ʌv·ən/ 44
over the weekend /oʊ·vər ðə 'wi·kend/ 16
overweight /,oʊ·vər'weɪt/ 32

package /'pæk·ɪdʒ/ 51
package tour /'pæk·ɪdʒ tʊr/ 50
painless /'peɪn·ləs/ 26
painting /peɪnt·ɪŋ/ 38
pair of boots /per ʌv buts/ 51
pajamas /pə'dʒam·əz/ 45
pale /peɪl/ 44
Panama /'pæ·nə·ma/ 36
panic /'pæn·ɪk/ 33
pants /pænts/ 31
pantyhose /'pænt·i,hoʊz/ 31
paper /'peɪ·pər/ 51
paper clip /'peɪ·pər klɪp/ 48
paper towel /'peɪ·pər 'taʊ·əl/ 44
paragraph /'pær·ə,græf/ 1
parakeet /'pær·ə,kit/ 40
parent /'pær·ənt/ 29
park /park/ 38
park a car /park ə kar/ 38
parking garage /'par·kɪŋ gə'raʒ/ 38
parrot /'pær·ət/ 40
party /'part·i/ 3
pass /pæs/ 14
pass your exam /pæs jʊr ɪg'zæm/ 48
passenger /'pæs·ən·dʒər/ 41
passport /'pæs·pɔrt/ 2, 41, 50
past /pæst/ 17
pasta /'pas·tə/ 43, 53
patents /'pæt·ənts/ 5
path /pæθ/ 39, 48
pay /peɪ/ 20, 42
pay a fine /peɪ ə faɪn/ 57
pay for /peɪ fɔr/ 24, 51
pay phone /peɪ foʊn/ 49
pea /pi/ 43
pear /per/ 43
pen /pen/ 51
pencil /'pen·səl/ 48
pencil sharpener /'pen·səl 'ʃar·pə·nər/ 48
people /'pi·pəl/ 36
perfect /'pɜr·fɪkt/ 22
period /'pɪr·i·əd/ 1
Peru /pə'ru/ 36
Peruvian /pə'ru·vi·ən/ 36
pet /pet/ 40
pharmacy /'far·mə·si/ 51
Philippines /'fɪl·ə'pinz/ 36

phone /foʊn/ 46
phone a friend /foʊn ə frend/ 12
phone book /foʊn bʊk/ 46
phone number /foʊn 'nʌm·bər/ 49
photocopier /'foʊt·ə,kap·i·ər/ 26, 59
phrasal verb /'freɪ·zəl vɜrb/ 11
phrase /freɪz/ 1
phrase book /freɪz bʊk/ 50
physical education /'fɪz·ɪ·kəl ,edʒ·ə'keɪ·ʃən/ 48
physics /'fɪz·ɪks/ 48
picture /'pɪk·tʃər/ 2, 26, 46
pie /paɪ/ 53
piece of paper /pis ʌv 'peɪ·pər/ 48
pig /pɪg/ 40
piglet /'pɪg·lət/ 40
pillow /'pɪl·oʊ/ 45
pineapple /'paɪ,næp·əl/ 43
Ping-Pong /'pɪŋ·pɔŋ/ 54
pizza /'pit·sə/ 43
plain /pleɪn/ 53
plane /pleɪn/ 41
plant /plænt/ 39, 59
plate /pleɪt/ 21
platform /'plæt·fɔrm/ 41
play /pleɪ/ 5, 55, 56
please /pliz/ 13, 35
plural /'plʊr·əl/ 1
police /pə'lis/ 57
police officer /pə'lis 'ɔ·fə·sər/ 38
Polish /'poʊl·ɪʃ/ 36
polite /pə'laɪt/ 25
politely /pə'laɪt·li/ 19
politics /'pal·ə,tɪks/ 26
pollution /pə'lu·ʃən/ 33, 60
poor /pʊr/ 60
pop /pap/ 43, 53
pork /pɔrk/ 40
Portuguese /,pɔr·tʃu'gis/ 36
positive /'paz·ət·ɪv/ 23
possible /'pas·ə·bəl/ 25
post office /poʊst 'ɔ·fəs/ 38, 51
postcard /'poʊst·kard/ 10, 50
pot /pat/ 44
potato /pə'teɪt·oʊ/ 43, 53
pound /paʊnd/ 21, 32
pre-exam /'pri·ɪg,zæm/ 25
prefer /prɪ'fɜr/ 34
preposition /,prep·ə'zɪʃ·ən/ 1
preschool /'pri·skul/ 25
present /'prez·ənt/ 17, 51
pretty /'prɪt·i/ 32
pretty good /'prɪt·i gʊd/ 35
prison /'prɪz·ən/ 57
problems /'prab·ləmz/ 59
product /'prad·əkt/ 40
professor /prə'fes·ər/ 48
program /'proʊ·græm/ 56, 58
proud of /praʊd ʌv/ 24
psychology /saɪ'kal·ə·dʒi/ 26
public /'pʌb·lɪk/ 42

Tourist Information Office
/'tʊr·əst ˌɪn·fər'meɪ·ʃən 'ɔ·fəs/
38, 50
Tourist Information Center
/'tʊr·əst ˌɪn·fər'meɪ·ʃən
sent·ər/ 50
towel /'taʊ·əl/ 45
town /taʊn/ 39
toy store /tɔɪ stɔr/ 51
toys /tɔɪz/ 51
tractor /'træk·tər/ 39
traffic /'træf·ɪk/ 21
traffic fumes /'træf·ɪk fjumz/ 33
traffic jam /'træf·ɪk dʒæm/ 24, 34, 60
train /treɪn/ 4, 41
train station /treɪn 'steɪ·ʃən/ 38
transportation /ˌtræn·spər'teɪ·ʃən/ 41, 50
travel /'træv·əl/ 2, 21, 41
traveler /'træv·ə·lər/ 26
traveler's check /'træv·ə·lərz tʃek/ 50, 52
trip /trɪp/ 41
tropical /'trɑp·ɪ·kəl/ 33
trunk /trʌŋk/ 2
try it on /traɪ ɪt ɑn/ 51
T-shirt /'ti·ʃɜrt/ 31, 51
Tuesday /'tuz·deɪ/ 16
Turkish /'tɜrk·ɪʃ/ 36
turn down /tɜrn daʊn/ 11
turn off /tɜrn ɔf/ 45
turn off the radio /tɜrn ɔf ðə 'reɪd·i‚oʊ/ 46
turn on /tɜrn ɑn/
turn on the light /tɜrn ɑn ðə laɪt/ 46
turn on the TV /tɜrn ɑn ðə ˌti'vi/ 46
turn up /tɜrn ʌp/ 10, 11
turtle /'tɜrt·əl/ 40
TV /ˌti'vi/ 46, 51, 52, 56, 58, 59
twice a day /twaɪs ə deɪ/ 17
twice a week /twaɪs ə wik/ 14
typically /'tɪp·ɪ·kli/ 12

ugly /'ʌg·li/ 32
umbrella /ʌm'brel·ə/ 31
unattractive /ˌʌn·ə'træk·tɪv/ 32
uncle /'ʌŋ·kəl/ 29
uncountable /ʌn·'kaʊnt·ə·bəl/ 21
under /'ʌn·dər/ 2, 46
understand /ˌʌn·dər'stænd/ 20
unemployed /ˌʌn·ɪm'plɔɪd/ 60
unfinished /ʌn'fɪn·ɪʃd/ 25
unfriendly /ʌn'fren·dli/ 19
unhappy /ʌn'hæp·i/ 19, 23, 25
United States /jʊ'naɪt·əd steɪts/ 36
university /ˌju·nə'vɜr·sət·i/ 48
unread /ʌn'red/ 25
unsafe /ʌn'seɪf/ 25

upset /ʌp'set/ 34
used to /juz tu/ 24
useful /'jus·fəl/ 21, 26
useless /'ju·sləs/ 26
usually /'ju·ʒə·wə·li/ 12, 17

vacation /veɪ'keɪ·ʃən/ 50
vandal /'væn·dəl/ 57
vandalism /'væn·dəlˌɪz·əm/ 57
vanilla /və'nɪl·ə/ 53
VCR /ˌvi·si'ɑr/ 40
veal /vil/ 40
vegetable /'vedʒ·tə·bəl/ 33, 43, 53, 56
vegetarian /ˌvedʒ·ə'ter·i·ən/ 53
Venezuela /ˌven·ə'zweɪ·lə/ 36
Venezuelan /ˌven·ə'zweɪ·lən/ 36
verb /vɜrb/ 1
very well /'ver·i wel/ 33
video /'vɪd·iˌoʊ/ 55, 56
videocassette recorder
/'vɪd·iˌoʊ·kə'set rɪ'kɔrd·ər/ 48
Vietnam /vi'ət'nɑm/ 36
Vietnamese /vi·ət·nɑ'miz/ 36
village /'vɪl·ɪdʒ/ 39
violent /'vaɪ·ə·lənt/ 25
visa /'vi·zə/ 50
visit /'vɪz·ət/ 4
vocabulary /voʊ'kæb·jəˌler·i/ 48
volleyball /'vɑl·iˌbɔl/ 54
vomit /'vɑm·ət/ 33

waist /weɪst/ 30
wait for /weɪt fɔr/ 24
waiter /'weɪt·ər/ 47
waitress /'weɪ·trəs/ 47
wake /weɪk/ 20
wake up /weɪk ʌp/ 12, 45
wake-up call /'weɪk·ʌp kɔl/ 52
walk (n.) /wɔk/ 40
walk (v.) /wɔk/ 14
wall /wɔl/ 46
want /wɑnt/ 34
want someone to /wɑnt 'sʌm·wən tu/ 34
warm /wɔrm/ 2, 34
washing machine /wɑʃ·ɪŋ mə'ʃin/ 59
waste /weɪst/ 60
watch /wɑtʃ/ 55, 56
watch a video /wɑtʃ ə 'vɪd·iˌoʊ/ 56
watch TV /wɑtʃ ˌti'vi/ 12, 46, 56
water (n.) /'wɔt·ər/ 2, 21, 60
water (v.) /'wɔt·ər/ 59
way /weɪ/ 19
wear /wer/ 20, 31
weather /'weð·ər/ 2, 21, 26, 37
wedding /'wed·ɪŋ/ 28
Wednesday /'wenz·deɪ/ 16
week /wik/ 16, 17
weekend /'wi·kend/ 16

weigh /weɪ/ 28, 32
weight /weɪt/ 32
well /wel/ 10, 19
well behaved /wel bɪ'heɪvd/ 23
well-done /ˌwel'dʌn/ 53
western /'wes·tərn/ 55
wet /wet/ 2, 10, 37
what time /wʌt taɪm/ 12
what do you do /wʌt du ju du/ 47
what's at the movies /wʌts æt ðə 'mu·viz/ 55
what's your job /wʌts jʊr dʒab/ 47
wheel /wil/ 2
when /wen/ 15
where /wer/ 13
where does /wer dʌz/ 44
where is /wer ɪz/ 38
why /waɪ/ 13
widow /'wɪd·oʊ/ 28
widowed /'wɪd·oʊd/ 28
widower /'wɪd·ə·wər/ 28
wife /waɪf/ 29
wild /waɪld/ 40
wildlife /'waɪld·laɪf/ 39
win /wɪn/ 20
wind /wɪnd/ 37
window /'wɪn·doʊ/ 2
windshield /'wɪnd·ʃild/ 2
windy /'wɪn·di/ 36
winter /'wɪnt·ər/ 16
winter vacation /'wɪnt·ər veɪ'keɪ·ʃən/ 50
women /'wʊm·ən/ 42, 58
wonderful /'wʌn·dər·fəl/ 22, 23
woods /wʊdz/ 39
wool /wʊl/ 40
word family /wɜrd 'fæm·ə·li/ 2
word processor /wɜrd 'prɑsˌes·ər/ 26
words /wɜrdz/ 1, 2
work (n.) /wɜrk/ 12, 21, 33
work (v.) /wɜrk/ 47, 59
worker /'wɜr·kər/ 26
worse /wɜrs/ 22
worst /wɜrst/ 22
would like /wʊd laɪk/ 34
write /raɪt/ 20, 48
write down /raɪt daʊn/ 2
write letters /raɪt 'let·ərz/ 12
wrong /rɔŋ/ 19

year /jɪr/ 16, 17
yesterday /'jes·tər·deɪ/ 16
young /jʌŋ/ 32
younger /'jʌŋ·gər/ 32
your /jʊr/ 30

zoo /zu/ 40
zoology /zoʊ'ɑl·ə·dʒi/ 26, 137

Answer Key

Unit 1

1.1 Check your work with a teacher if you are not sure about your answers.

1.2

Noun	Verb	Adjective
shirt	speak	bad
car	have	new
banana	write	old
woman	eat	sad

1.3 *Possible answers:*
on, by, at, of, to, for, with, below, through, from, in

1.4 2. question   5. question
3. phrase   6. sentence
4. sentence

1.5 2. woman   4. No, it's a noun.
3. No, it's a preposition.   5. No, it's a sentence.

1.6 *Possible answers:*
1. is
2. black, green, blue, red (*or* yellow, orange, etc.)
3. speak, English
4. make a mistake; do homework; take a shower

Unit 2

2.1 *Possible answers:*
have a party, have lunch, have a class, have a cup of coffee, have a meeting, etc.

2.2
wet
dry
warm ———— weather
cool
rainy

2.3

Name of word family	Words in family
education	school, teacher, notebook, exam, student
food and drink	bread, milk, water, salad, rice

2.4 *Possible pictures:*

1. a plane **lands**

2. **sunny weather**

3. **under** the table

2.5 *Possible words:*

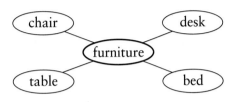

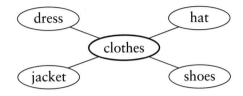

Unit 3

3.1 *Suggested answers:*

2. appointment   4. party   6. cold   8. baby
3. exam   5. time   7. date

3.2 *Possible answers:*

1. Yes, I have two brothers and a sister.
2. I have to go to class on Mondays and Wednesdays.   *or*   I don't have to go to class at all.
3. I usually have a sandwich or a salad.
4. I don't have to get up early on weekends.   *or*   On weekends I have to get up early to go to work.   *or*   I like to get up early on weekends, but I don't have to.
5. I sometimes have arguments with my friends, but not very often.
6. I have an old bicycle, a computer that doesn't work, clothes that I never wear, etc.
7. I have my hair cut about once a month.
8. Sometimes I have trouble understanding English when people talk very fast.

3.3 *Across*
1. meal
3. party
5. snack

Down
2. exams
4. tea

¹M	²E	A	L	
	X			
³P	A	R	⁴T	Y
	M	■	E	■
	⁵S	N	A	C	K

3.4 *Suggested answers:*

1. Why don't you have something to drink / have a drink / have a cup of coffee / have a cup of tea?
2. Have a good trip! / Have a good time!
3. Have you got a minute?

Unit 4

4.1 2. Jean and Mike **are going shopping.**
      3. Antonio **is going to Rome.**
      4. The Lees **are going to the beach.**
      5. Sun-hee **is going fishing.**

4.2 2. We're going **sightseeing** today.
      3. Joe went **up** to the top of the hill.   *or*   Joe went down to the **bottom** of the hill.
      4. Let's go **shopping** today.
      5. Sarah went out **of** the shop.

4.3 *Possible answers:*

I sometimes go swimming.   I never go skiing.
I sometimes go dancing.   I never go fishing.
I always go sightseeing.

4.4 2. On Tuesday Sue is going to write to Luis.
      3. On Wednesday she is going to watch the World Cup on TV.
      4. On Thursday she is going to have her hair cut.
      5. On Friday she is going to go to the movies.

4.5 *Possible answers:*

From New York, trains go to Boston and to Washington, D.C. Buses go to Albany and to Buffalo. Roads go to New Jersey and to Connecticut from New York.

Unit 5

5.1 2. What is the woman doing? She's reading a book.
      3. What are the girls doing? They're playing tennis.
      4. What is the man in the house doing? He's doing the dishes.
      5. What is the dog doing? It's sleeping.

5.2 2. What does Bill Atkins do? He's a teacher.
      3. What does Maria Santos do? She's a doctor.
      4. What do Ted and Kumiko do? They're students.

5.3 2. What did Bill Atkins do? He taught three lessons.
      3. What did Maria Santos do? She met with five patients.
      4. What did Ted and Kumiko do? They wrote essays.

5.4 *Possible answers:*

I usually do the dishes.
My husband and I both do the laundry.
My husband does exercises every morning.
My wife does business with Argentina.
I hate doing the housework.
I love doing the cooking.
My mother always does a good job.

Unit 6

6.1   2. do   3. make   4. make   5. do

6.2   1. That movie made/makes me sad.   *or*   That movie made/makes me feel sad.
2. Exams at school always make/made me nervous.   *or*   Exams at school always make/made me feel nervous.
3. The salesclerk wasn't very nice to me; it made/makes me angry.   *or* . . . it made/makes me feel angry

6.3   1. She's making a photocopy.
2. She's making tea.
3. He's making a phone call / a telephone call.
4. They're making a video / a movie.

6.4   2. Can I **take** a photo of you?
3. He's 35, but he never **does** his own laundry. He takes his dirty clothes to his mother's.
4. I have to **make** an appointment with the dentist.
5. Do students have to **take** an exam at the end of their English course?
6. Yes or no? We have to **make** a decision today.

Unit 7

7.1   2. back / home / back home   4. How
3. from   5. back/home

7.2   *Possible answers:*
1. I usually come home at 5:30.
2. I'm from / I come from Japan/Chile/Toronto/Bangkok/San Juan/Hong Kong, etc.
3. I sit down and talk to my friends / take out my books.

7.3   *Suggested answers:*
1. Come in!
2. We're going to have a barbecue at home this weekend. Would you like to come over?

7.4   1. came   2. come   3. comes   4. coming / going to come   5. came

7.5   *Possible answers (These definitions and examples are from the* Cambridge Dictionary of American English*):*
1. **come across** | FIND | can mean "to find something or someone by chance."
He came across some of his old love letters.
2. **come on** | HURRY | can mean "to move or act quickly or more quickly."
Come on – we're going to be late if you don't hurry!
3. **come up** | BE MENTIONED | can mean "to be mentioned or talked about in conversation."
What points came up at the meeting?

Unit 8

8.1   *Possible answers:*
1. It takes me 15 minutes to get to school/class.
2. It takes me 3 hours to go from New York to Washington, D.C.
3. It takes me an hour to do one unit of this book.

8.2   1. take an exam   3. take your driving test
2. took a course / am taking a course

8.3   *Suggested answers:*
1. She takes the train.
2. You can / could / should / have to take a taxi.
3. He takes the school bus / the bus.
4. They take the subway.

8.4   *Suggested answers:*
2. I take an umbrella.
3. I take my passport.
4. I take my notebook / my books and some pens/pencils.

8.5   *Possible answer:*
It took me about an hour to do this unit.

Unit 9

9.1   2. bring   3. bring   4. Take   5. take

9.2   1. take; bring . . . back   2. brought . . . back   3. take; bring . . . back

9.3   2. c   3. b   4. a   5. d

9.4   1. brought   2. brought   3. took   4. took . . . bring

9.5   *Possible answers:*
(a) I always bring my notebook, pen, and dictionary to class.
(b) I always take my English book, tape recorder, and cassettes to class.

9.6   My parents brought me some handkerchiefs, CDs, and chocolates from their last trip.

Unit 10

10.1   *Suggested answers:*
1. (b) tired   2. (c) sick   3. (a) hot

10.2   *Suggested answers:*
2. gets light / will get light   4. I'm getting wet!
3. he's getting better / he'll get better   5. I'm getting cold.

10.3   *Suggested answers:*
2. a job   4. a newspaper
3. a pen/pencil and paper   5. a taxi

10.4   1. gets to   2. gets to   3. can I get to / do I get to

10.5 *Possible answers:*

1. In the U.S. and Canada, many people get married when they are 20 to 30 years old.
2. People usually get married on weekends, often on Saturday. The summer months (June, July, and August) are very popular.
3. I get home at about 6 o'clock. I get there / I get home by bus.

Unit 11

11.1   2. f   3. e   4. b   5. d   6. a

11.2   2. off   4. off   6. along   8. on
          3. on; up   5. off   7. up

11.3   2. The alarm clock is going off.
          3. The man is getting up.
          4. The woman is turning on the oven.

11.4 *Possible answers:*
There are lots of different ways to answer this question. Here is one way:

Words connected with getting dressed and daily routine
put on clothes (e.g., a coat)
take off clothes (e.g., shoes)
get up

Words connected with movement
come on
take off (airplane)

Words connected with equipment
turn up (TV, stereo)
turn down
turn on
turn off
go off

Words connected with people or events
get along
going on
get over
turn down (an offer)
come up

11.5   2. going on   3. Turn up the radio.   4. got over

Unit 12

12.1   *Possible answers:*

1. I usually wake up at 7 o'clock on weekdays.
2. I usually have coffee and toast for breakfast.
3. I normally go to work by car/train/subway/bus.   *or*   I normally go to work on foot.
4. I usually have a cup of coffee/tea at 11 o'clock.
5. I usually take a shower at about 8 a.m.   *or*   I usually take a bath at about 10 p.m.

12.2   2. He does the laundry every Saturday.
3. She cleans the house every weekend.
4. He watches TV/television every evening.
5. She goes for a walk every Sunday.

12.3   *Suggested questions:*

2. How often do you go for a walk?
3. How do you go to work?
4. When do you have dinner?

Unit 13

13.1   *Suggested answers:*

2. told   3. said   4. tell; said   5. tell   6. said

Note: Other verb tenses may be possible; e.g., I *will say* good-bye to him.

13.2   2. How do you say "tea" in Chinese?
3. Excuse me, can you tell me the time? / . . . can you tell me what time it is?
4. Can you tell me when the exam is?
5. Can you answer the phone/telephone, please?

13.3   2. Answer the door.
3. Ask for the check.
4. Reply to a letter.
5. Say happy birthday.
6. Talk to a friend.
7. Ask someone to help you.

Note: We can say *answer a letter* but not *reply to the door*!

13.4   1. c   2. d   3. a   4. b

Unit 14

14.1   *Suggested answers:*

2. danced   4. run   6. fell   8. walk
3. swims   5. climb   7. jumped; swam

14.2   2. flies   4. drives   6. ride
3. take   5. take/ride; go by

Note: You can also use *go by* with most of these forms of transportation (but without *the* or *a*); e.g., you can *go* to work *by* bicycle, *go* home *by* subway/taxi/bus, etc.)

14.3 *Possible answers:*

2. I ride my bike twice a week.
3. I swim in the ocean once a year.
   I never swim in a pool.
4. I never go jogging. / I never jog.

5. I drive a car every day.
6. I go dancing once a month.

14.4 *Possible answers:*

Please pass the salt.
Please pass the pepper.
Please pass the bread.

Please pass the water.
Please pass the salad.
Please pass the sauce.

14.5

2. Mei-Li drove her grandmother to the mall yesterday.
3. Maria caught the 8:45 train to the city yesterday.
4. I took a taxi home from the train station yesterday.
5. Tom fell when he rode his bike yesterday.

Unit 15

15.1 2. and 3. before 4. so 5. although 6. if

15.2 *Possible sentences:*

Mary agreed to marry Paul after they decided to go into business together.
Mary will marry Paul although/though she doesn't love him.
Mary agreed to marry Paul, and they had two sons.
Mary agreed to marry Paul because he was a rock star.
Mary will marry Paul before he moves to Hollywood.
Mary will marry Paul, but she doesn't love him.
Mary agreed to marry Paul if he moved to Hollywood.
Mary agreed to marry Paul, so he moved to Hollywood.
Mary will marry Paul when he moves to Hollywood.

15.3 Check with a teacher or a dictionary if you are not sure if your answers are correct.

15.4 1. as well / too / also 2. Even 3. like 4. Only 5. than

15.5 *Possible answers:*

I play tennis only in the summer.
It is too cold to swim here even in summer.
She plays the piano better than I do.
He swims like a fish.
I like listening to music, and I like reading also.
I like going skiing too.
I go skiing a lot with the children, and sometimes my husband comes as well.

15.6 *Possible answers:*

1. . . . I enjoy it.
2. . . . I do all the exercises in this book.
3. . . . I am also studying French.
4. . . . it is difficult at times.
5. . . . I was twelve.
6. . . . I can understand some English-language movies.

Unit 16

16.1   2. a century   3. a week   4. a year

16.2   (a) Sunday, Monday, Tuesday, Wednesday, Thursday, Friday, Saturday
    (b) January, February, March, April, May, June, July, August, September,
        October, November, December

16.3   Thirty days has **September,**
    April, June, and **November.**
    All the rest have **thirty-one,**
    Except for **February** alone:
    Which has but **twenty-eight,** in fine,
    Till leap year gives it **twenty-nine.**

    This is a traditional rhyme that people use to help them remember the number of days
    of the month. It means that:
    September, April, June, and November each have thirty days. The other months have
    thirty-one days except for February, which has twenty-eight days, and twenty-nine
    days in a leap year. Leap year takes place once every four years.

16.4   1. Monday   5. Wednesday   9. February
    2. August   6. January   10. September
    3. October   7. April   11. Tuesday
    4. Saturday   8. Thursday   12. November

16.5   1. T F S (first letters of the days of the week)
    2. A S O N D (first letters of the months)

16.6   I'm going to a party on <u>Saturday</u> for Jill's birthday. Her birthday is on <u>Tuesday</u>,
    but she wanted to have the party on the <u>weekend</u>. She's having a barbecue. I think
    spring is a good time to have a party because of the weather. I love going to
    barbecues <u>in</u> the spring. My birthday is in <u>winter</u>, and it's too cold to eat outside!

16.7   *Possible answers:*
    It is possible here to give answers to only some of these questions. Check with your
    teacher if you are not sure of the answers to any of the other questions.

    1. 900   5. July   7. The 21st century   8. 30

Unit 17

17.1   2. for   3. from   4. to   5. At   6. for

17.2   1. Probably tomorrow.   2. Probably a week ago.   3. In a few minutes.

17.3   *Possible answers:*
    2. I sometimes go to school by bus. I usually go by car.
    3. I never play soccer.
    4. I always watch TV at night.
    5. I occasionally drink milk. I usually drink coffee.
    6. I never wear a hat.
    7. I often eat chocolate.
    8. I sometimes go to bed at 10. I usually go to bed at 11.
    9. I sometimes go to the theater.

17.4 John plays tennis twice a week. He practices the piano once a week, and he has a business meeting in Toronto once a month.

Sally and Amy play tennis three times a week. They practice the piano twice a day. They go to Toronto for a business meeting six times a year. *or* They have a business meeting in Toronto six times a year.

17.5 *Possible answer:*
I usually get up early. I always have a cup of coffee when I wake up. I often work at home, but sometimes I go to a school to teach. I never drive. Sometimes I walk to school, and sometimes I go by bus. Sometimes I have lunch in a park near school. I usually eat a sandwich, and occasionally I have an apple too, but I hardly ever have a hot lunch. Once a week I visit a friend, and we go to the movies together or have lunch in a restaurant.

Unit 18

18.1 1. here   2. there   3. here   4. there

18.2 1. back from Paris / home from Paris (*also*: back home from Paris)
2. everywhere (You can also say "all over.")

18.3 the top of the tree   the back of the bus

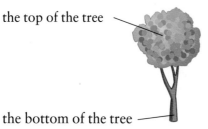

the side of the bus

the bottom of the tree   the front of the bus

18.4 *Possible answers:*
1. I'm studying English at home, in my country.
2. Yes, I'm going to Canada and to the U.S.
3. At the moment I have a pen in my right hand.
4. The unit on **Have** is at the beginning of this book (Unit 3). Note *at*.
5. The unit on **Feelings** is in the middle of this book (Unit 34). Note *in*.

18.5 1. abroad   2. out   3. away / out of town   4. away; abroad

Unit 19

19.1 2. badly   3. loudly   4. fast (*not* ~~fastly~~)   5. quietly   6. well

19.2 *Possible answers:*
1. Usually a quiet person is better.
2. Most people like a fast bus.
3. A friendly person!
4. A right answer is best in class!
5. To speak politely – always.
6. Usually it's better to speak in a normal way.

19.3

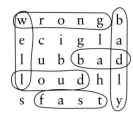

19.4

Word	Definition	Right (✓)	Wrong (✗)
suddenly	very slowly		✗
sadly	in an unhappy way	✓	
strangely	not in a normal way	✓	
quickly	very slowly		✗
easily	with no difficulty	✓	

Suddenly means very quickly, when you are not expecting it.
Quickly is similar to "fast" when *fast* is an adverb (e.g., He runs *fast*.), not when it is an adjective.

19.5 *Possible answers:*

My cousin runs fast.   My mother is very friendly.
My aunt is a quiet person.   My father drives well.
My brother speaks slowly.   I'm a fast runner.

Unit 20

20.2 *Suggested answers:*

2. give, gave, given; opposite – take, took, taken
3. come, came, come; opposite – go, went, gone
4. throw, threw, thrown; opposite – catch, caught, caught
5. sit, sat, sat; opposite – stand, stood, stood
6. arrive, arrived, arrived; opposite – leave, left, left
7. remember, remembered, remembered; opposite – forget, forgot, forgotten
8. rise, rose, risen; opposite – fall, fell, fallen
9. win, won, won; opposite – lose, lost, lost
10. buy, bought, bought; opposite – sell, sold, sold

20.3 *Suggested answers:*

2. ate/had   5. drove/went   8. bought   11. left   14. slept
3. made/had   6. wrote   9. sat   12. met
4. read   7. ran/jogged   10. made   13. went

20.4 *Suggested answers:*

2. been   3. had/eaten   4. spent   5. known   6. seen

Unit 21

21.1 2. milk; butter   3. advice   4. traffic   5. work

21.2 *Suggested answers:*
1. heavy traffic / heavy furniture
2. useful information / useful news
3. bad news / bad traffic / bad information
4. modern furniture
5. fried rice
6. cold water / cold rice
7. space travel

There may be other possible answers, depending on the context.

21.3 *Possible answers:*

brown sugar; heavy traffic; good advice; fresh air; hard work; delicious spaghetti; unsalted butter; cold milk; herbal tea; black coffee

21.4
2. is/was
3. are/were
4. is/was
5. is / was / will be; was
6. are
7. is/was

21.5
2. I'd like some <u>information</u> about your country.
3. Let me give you <u>some</u> advice.
4. Cook <u>this</u> rice for thirty minutes.
5. Mary is looking for a new <u>job</u>.
6. There's usually better weather in the east than in the west.
7. We should buy some new <u>furniture</u>.
8. We went on two long <u>trips</u> last year.

Unit 22

22.1 *Possible answers:*
2. great/wonderful/terrific
3. terrible/awful/bad
4. excellent/great/wonderful
5. awful/terrible
6. wonderful/great

22.2 *Possible answers:*
2. Oh, how awful!
3. That's a great/good idea. *or* Yes, great!
4. Yes, there's the Ritz. It's the best restaurant in town.
5. She's/He's a wonderful person! (We hope you can say this!)
6. How disgusting!

22.3 2. e 3. f 4. a 5. b 6. d

22.4

good (+)	bad (−)
fabulous	dreadful
fine	horrendous
gorgeous	horrible
superb	

22.5 *Possible answers:*

fabulous weather / a fabulous vacation
a fine person / a fine time
a gorgeous view / gorgeous clothes
a superb idea / a superb dinner

a horrendous crime / a horrendous experience
a horrible accident / a horrible feeling

Unit 23

23.1 *Suggested answers:*

1. A: Mary's very nice.
   B: She's more than nice, she's **wonderful!**
2. A: George wasn't very nice to you, was he?
   B: He was really **awful/nasty!**
3. A: Let me carry your bag.
   B: Thanks, that's (very) **kind/thoughtful** of you.
4. A: Is your little brother a good boy?
   B: Yes, he's very **well behaved.**

23.2

1. happy	3. easygoing	5. unhappy	7. selfish	9. thoughtful
2. wonderful	4. good	6. difficult	8. stupid	10. nice

```
    1            2
    H            W
3
E  A  S  Y  G  O  I  N  G⁴
   P         N        O
   P         D        O
   Y         E        D
             R     U⁵ ■ D⁶   S⁷
          S⁸ F     N  ■ I    E
          T⁹ H  O  U  G  H  T  F  U  L
             U    L  A     F    F
             P       P     I    I
         N¹⁰ I  C  E  P     C    S
             D       Y     U    H
                           L
                           T
```

23.3 Most people probably think they are most of these things at some time, or at least the positive ones!

23.4 2. of   3. to   4. of

Unit 24

24.1 2. e   3. a   4. f   5. d   6. b

24.2 *Possible answers:*

2. for them   4. for a new one   6. up a (new) word
3. at me   5. forward to it

24.3 1. to   2. at   3. to   4. in   5. to   6. of

24.4   3. He wasn't used to eating American food.
         4. He wasn't used to speaking English every day.
         5. He was used to expensive stores.
         6. He wasn't used to American money.

24.5   *Possible answers:*
         1. I was good at languages and bad at sports.
         2. I usually ask for a black coffee.
         3. I am proud of my family.
         4. I am afraid of going to the dentist.
         5. I like listening to jazz.
         6. I am looking forward to my vacation.
         7. I belong to a health/fitness club.
         8. I am used to eating lots of different kinds of food.

Unit 25

25.1   2. rewrite/redo   4. unhappy   6. unsafe
         3. informal   5. misbehave

25.2   *Possible answers:*
       He and his ex-wife are good friends.
       It is impossible to read his handwriting.
       I like my new boss much better than my ex-boss.
       Preschool children learn by playing.
       This work is not very good. Please redo it.

25.3   *Suggested answers:*
         2. nerves (or nervousness) before an exam
         3. a wrong answer, an answer that is not correct
         4. a book that has not been read
         5. to tell a story again
         6. a word that is not spelled correctly
         7. a letter that is not finished
         8. a drink with no alcohol in it (for example, fruit juice, cola)
         9. to read a book for a second time
       10. to make an audiotape or videotape go backward, using a machine

25.4   *Possible answers:*
       im: an impolite question   pre: prepaid tickets
       mis: to misjudge someone   re: to repaint a room
       non: a nonstick pan   un: an unanswered question

25.5   *Possible answer:*
       This paragraph is a silly story, but it uses most of the words in the chart.

       He is a very **unhappy** ex-president. He never sees his **ex-wife** because she
       misunderstands everything he says. He doesn't visit his **preschool** grandchildren
       because they live in an **unsafe** area. It is very crowded there and it is **impossible** for
       nonresidents to park there. He is **rewriting** his autobiography for the third time in a
       very **informal** style. I don't know why he **redoes** it so often.

25.6   2. uncomfortable   4. inconvenient   6. unsure   8. incorrect
         3. unfriendly   5. nonviolent   7. impolite

Unit 26

26.1   2. happily   3. instructor   4. word processor   5. swimmer   6. useful

26.2   *Possible answers:*

(You may be able to think of some other possible combinations.)
2. useless idea / book / car
3. beautiful picture / beach / book / weather / smile / car
4. sandy beach
5. sunny weather
6. hard worker
7. useful idea / book / car
8. endless beach / fun / book

26.3   1. politics   2. sociology   3. economics   4. psychology

26.4   Check with a teacher if you are not sure if your answers are right or not.

26.5   *Suggested answers:*

2. a person who travels
3. the opposite of quickly
4. with lots of hope
5. weather when it is raining
6. It doesn't hurt.
7. the opposite of doing something well
8. a thing (or gadget) for opening cans
9. the study of numbers and amounts
10. a person who surfs

Unit 27

27.1   2. lose   3. felt   4. fell   5. quite   6. loose

27.2   1. a   2. b   3. a   4. b

27.3   2. quiet
3. lost the tickets (for the concert)
4. afternoon
5. lend me 35 cents to make a phone call (please)
6. missed my train

27.4   *Possible answers:*

1. I am expecting my brother at 5:30. (He said he would come at 5:30.)
2. I hope to learn a lot of new words with this book. (I really want to learn new words with this book.)
3. Sometimes I borrow books and tapes.
4. Yes, but only my *best* friend!
5. I feel fine today. Yesterday I felt fine too.

Unit 28

28.1   *Possible answers:*

My mother was born in Hong Kong on April 19, 1957.
My father was born in Singapore on June 4, 1949.
My brother was born in Mexico City on June 6, 1980.
My husband was born in Taipei on February 6, 1969.
My son was born in Vancouver on October 16, 1998.

28.2
2. Diana, Princess of Wales, was born in 1961 and died in 1997.
3. Genghis Khan was born in 1162 and died in 1227.
4. Elvis Presley was born in 1935 and died in 1977.
5. Joan of Arc was born in 1412 and died in 1431.
6. Martin Luther King, Jr., was born in 1929 and died in 1968.

28.3 1. died   2. death   3. dead   4. died   5. dead

28.4
2. (bride)groom   6. a funeral
3. single   7. a honeymoon
4. to weigh 100 pounds   8. a widow (woman); a widower (man); or widowed
5. divorced

28.5 1. In   2. to   3. of   4. on   5. born   6. after

28.6 *Possible answer:*

I have two brothers and two sisters. My sisters are both married. One sister got married this year. She had a big wedding and was a beautiful bride. They went to Hawaii on their honeymoon. The other sister got married four years ago. She has two children – the boy was born two years ago, and the girl was born last year. One of my brothers is divorced and one is single. My father died two years ago. My mother is a widow.

Unit 29

29.1
2. brother   7. nephew
3. aunt   8. niece
4. uncle   9. mother
5. grandmother   10. wife
6. grandfather   11. cousin

29.2 *Possible family tree:*

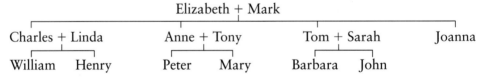

I am Tony. Anne is my wife. Peter and Mary are our children. Peter is our son, and Mary is our daughter. Barbara is our niece. William, Henry, and John are our nephews.

29.3
2. aunt   4. father   6. cousins   8. daughter
3. brother   5. grandsons   7. grandmother

29.4 *Possible answers:*
1. Chen has one brother and no sisters.
2. Chen has two cousins.
3. Chen has two nephews, but he doesn't have any nieces.
4. Chen has only one grandmother now.

Unit 30

30.1 2. heart   3. teeth   4. nose   5. toes   6. ears   7. brain   8. blood

30.2
1. (a) back   (b) arms   (c) legs
2. The eye is the hole in the needle.
3. The face is the front of the clock (with the numbers on it). The big hand that shows the minutes is pointing at 12, and the little hand that shows the hours is pointing at 3.
4. The neck is the narrow part at the top of the bottle.
5. The foot of the mountain is the bottom of the mountain (the lowest part).

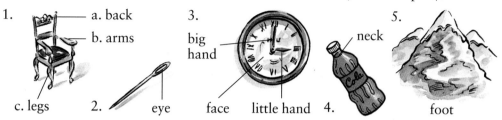

1.   a. back   b. arms   c. legs
2.   eye
3.   big hand   face   little hand
4.   neck
5.   foot

30.3   2. football   3. lipstick   4. hairbrush   5. earring   6. handbag

30.4   If you find you learned the words with the pictures particularly well, then try, whenever possible, to draw a picture next to words you want to learn.

Unit 31

31.1   All the words fit into both columns except for *tie* – men; *dress, skirt, pantyhose, handbag* – women.

31.2
1. foot – shoe
2. hand – glove
3. eyes – glasses
4. waist – belt
5. head – hat
6. neck – scarf

31.3
1. are; is
2. is wearing
3. has; is carrying
4. is; are
5. were; are
6. Is

31.4
2. sweater
3. gloves
4. skirt
5. boots
6. hat
7. shirt (*also:* blouse)
8. coat
9. briefcase
10. umbrella

31.5   *Possible answer:*

I am wearing a blue T-shirt and black pants. I have white shoes on. I'm also wearing gloves and a pair of glasses.

Unit 32

32.1
2. tall
3. slim/thin
4. light/fair
5. young
6. overweight/fat
7. elderly

32.2   *Suggested questions:*
2. Is Elena's hair blonde/fair/light?
3. Is Mike's hair long?
4. Are your parents old? (*or* more polite: Are your parents elderly?)
5. Why is Hiromi so thin? Why does Hiromi look so thin?

32.3 *Suggested answers:*

1. Sue has long blonde hair and fair/light skin. (*also:* a fair/light complexion)
2. Jeff has dark skin and short black hair.
3. Wendy has long dark hair.
4. Dick's hair is long, and he has a beard and a mustache.

32.4 *Possible answers:*

Lisa Chin: Lisa Chin is fairly tall. She has long black hair and brown eyes. She's very pretty.

Kevin: Kevin is medium height. He has brown hair and a beard. His eyes are blue. He's kind of ordinary looking.

My mother: My mother is short, with gray hair. She has green eyes. She is a beautiful woman.

Unit 33

33.1 *Suggested answers:*

Not very serious	Somewhat serious	Very serious
a headache a cold a toothache	allergies asthma	cancer cholera a heart attack malaria

Note: The health problems labeled "not very serious" and "somewhat serious" can become very serious if they are not treated.

33.2 *Suggested answers:*

1. (I'm) fine, thanks. / I'm very well, thank you.
2. I feel sick/ill.   *or*   I don't feel very well.
3. I feel sick/ill.   *or*   I don't feel well.
4. I have a toothache.
5. a cold?

33.3 *Possible answers:*

1. A lot of fruit and vegetables, not so many sweets.
2. I like/love swimming / cycling / playing golf / skiing / jogging / playing tennis, etc.
3. Sometimes I have a lot of stress at work / when I have exams.
4. Yes, I had an operation once / I broke my leg, etc. ("Be in **the** hospital" means you are a patient, staying in a hospital. "Be in **a** hospital" can mean that you are a patient or that you are visiting someone.)

33.4   2. cholera   4. allergies
           3. asthma   5. cancer / heart attacks (*also:* heart disease)

Unit 34

34.1 *Possible answers:*

2. I hate cowboy movies.   5. I love soccer.   8. I don't like jazz.
3. I like airplanes.   6. I don't like cats.
4. I like tea.   7. I like cars.

34.2 *Possible answers:*

2. I prefer cats to dogs.
3. I prefer shopping to sightseeing.
4. I prefer Toyotas to Fords.
5. I prefer strawberry to chocolate ice cream.
6. I prefer playing sports to watching sports.

34.3 *Possible answers:*

2. I hope (that) the lesson ends soon.
3. I want something to eat / some food.
4. I hope (that) my friend feels better soon.
5. I want to go to bed / go to sleep.
6. I hope to see my friend soon.   *or*   I hope (that) we see each other soon.

34.4

2. Fred is thirsty.
3. The children are happy.
4. Bob is tired.
5. Mr. Lee is cold.
6. Mrs. Jones is angry.

34.5 *Possible answers:*

2. I felt surprised yesterday when an old friend called me.
3. I felt upset when my boss was rude to me.

Note: You can also say: I was angry; I was surprised; I was upset.

Unit 35

35.1 *Suggested answers:*

2. Good luck!
3. Congratulations!
4. Good-bye. / See you soon. / Take care.
5. Happy Birthday!
6. Fine, thanks. / Pretty good.
7. Hello!/Hi!
8. Thank you. / Thanks.

35.2

1. Excuse me!
2. Congratulations!
3. Happy New Year!
4. Good morning.
5. I'm sorry.
6. Good night. / Take care. / See you soon.

35.3 *Suggested answers:*

2. Good night. Sleep well.
3. Good morning. (*also:* Hello.)
4. Happy New Year!
5. I'm sorry. / Excuse me. I didn't understand.

35.4

ANN: Hi.
BILL: Hi/Hello.
ANN: How are you?
BILL: Fine, thanks. How about you?*
ANN: It's my birthday today.
BILL: Happy Birthday!
ANN: Would you like something to drink?
BILL: Yes, please. A diet soda.
ANN: With ice?
BILL: No, thanks. / Yes, please.
ANN: Here you are.
BILL: Thank you.

* You can say "Terrible" as Bill did, but usually we say "Fine" even if we feel terrible.

35.5 *Possible answer:*

A: Good morning.
B: Hi. How are you?
A: Fine, thanks. How about you?
B: Pretty good, but I'm a little nervous. I'm taking my driving test today.
A: Good luck. That's funny, I passed mine last week.
B: Oh, congratulations!
A: It's my birthday today.
B: It is? Happy Birthday! Why don't we go out and celebrate this evening?
A: OK. See you later.
B: See you soon.

Unit 36

36.1
2. The Alps are in Europe.
3. The Amazon River is in South America.
4. The Great Barrier Reef is in Australia.
5. The Great Wall is in Asia.
6. The Andes Mountains are in South America.
7. The Nile River is in Africa.
8. Mount Fuji is in Asia.
9. The Grand Canyon is in North America.

36.2
2. Beijing – d. China
3. Seoul – g. South Korea
4. Bogotá – h. Colombia
5. Caracas – j. Venezuela
6. Washington, D.C. – i. the United States
7. Bangkok – a. Thailand
8. Buenos Aires – f. Argentina
9. Rome – b. Italy
10. Mexico City – c. Mexico

36.3 Check your answers with your teacher or a reference book (such as an atlas or a dictionary) if you are not sure.

36.4
2. In Mexico, Spain, and Panama they speak Spanish, but in Brazil they speak Portuguese.
3. In Austria, Germany, and Switzerland they speak German, but in Italy they speak Italian.
4. In Taiwan, China, and Singapore they speak Chinese, but in Japan they speak Japanese.

36.5
2. Thai
3. Egyptian
4. Brazilian
5. Canadian
6. Mexican
7. Filipino
8. French
9. Peruvian
10. Chinese
11. Vietnamese
12. Indonesian
13. Chilean

Unit 37

37.1 1. e   2. d   3. g   4. a   5. f   6. b   7. c

37.2 *Possible answer:*
most favorite ←————————→ least favorite
snow, sun, wind, rain, lightning, cloud, fog

37.3
3. It is cloudy in Caracas.
4. It is snowing / It is snowy in London.
5. It is foggy in Seoul.
6. It is windy in Toronto.

37.4
2. rains / is raining
3. weather
4. snowing/snowy
5. lightning
6. storm/thunderstorm/hurricane

37.5 *Possible answers:*
1. It sometimes snows in December.
2. It is usually 70 degrees Fahrenheit in summer and 32 degrees Fahrenheit in winter.
3. Sometimes there are thunderstorms in August.
4. It is not usually wet in spring.
5. We almost never have hurricanes.
6. Summer is my favorite season because it is warm and dry.

37.6 *Possible answer:*
Today it is sunny and warm. There are just a few clouds in the sky and a little wind. It is not raining, and it is not snowing. There is no thunder or lightning.

Unit 38

38.1
2. At the tourist information office.
3. At the bank.
4. In/At the parking garage.
5. At the museum.
6. At the post office.
7. At the bookstore.
8. At the library.

38.2 *Possible questions:*
2. Where's the post office?
3. How do I get to the art museum?
4. Where can I park? *or* What's the best place to park?
5. Where can I change money? *or* Is there a bank nearby?

38.3 *Suggested answers:*
2. at a store
3. at the library
4. on the street *or* in a police station
5. in a bank

38.4
1. Railroad crossing
2. Bus stop
3. No parking (Do not leave your car here.)
4. Information
5. Airport ahead

38.5 *Suggested answers:*
I live in a small town. It has a bank and a post office, but no library and no parking garage. The police officer knows everyone who lives there.

Unit 39

39.1
1. mountains
2. forest
3. lake
4. hills
5. town or village
6. path
7. woods
8. fields
9. river
10. farm
11. road
12. tractor

39.2 *Suggested answers:*
1. on
2. cabin
3. town/village
4. mountains
5. lake/river (*also:* pond, swimming pool)
6. wildlife
7. path

39.3 *Possible sentences:*

1. There are some big forests and a lot of farms.
2. There are no hills or mountains. The countryside is flat. There are a lot of paths where you can walk.
3. There is one big river and some small rivers. The wildlife there is very beautiful.
4. There are a lot of villages and some small towns.

39.4 1. He loves nature.
2. She wants to live in the country.
3. They are interested in wildlife.

Unit 40

40.1 *Suggested answers:*

2. giraffe
3. Parrots; parakeets; chickens
4. Tigers; lions
5. horse; elephant
6. Fish; birds
7. meat
8. Chickens; cows (*or* pigs)

40.2 2. calf – e. veal   3. lamb – a. lamb   4. cow – c. beef   5. pig – b. ham

40.3 *Possible answers:*

1. Lions, tigers, monkeys, snakes, dogs, and cats.
2. Cows, sheep, pigs, parrots (for feathers), and snakes (for snakeskin). (You may think of some other things, e.g., horsehair for certain wigs).
3. Chickens, turtles, parrots, parakeets, snakes, and fish.

40.4

Across	Down
3. cats	1. parrot
6. lion	2. monkey
7. horse	4. sheep
8. elephant	5. tiger

40.5 Write down the number you remembered correctly. Try again tomorrow and write down how many you remember then.

Unit 41

41.1 2. d   4. f   6. g
3. a   5. c   7. b

41.2 1. A one-way ticket takes you to a place, and a round-trip ticket takes you to a place and back.
2. You get your luggage/baggage [bags and suitcases].
3. No, it lands at the end of a trip and takes off at the beginning of a trip.
4. If you rent a car, you use it for a day or a week and then return it. If you buy a car, it is your car.
5. No, you want them to take you somewhere in their car.

41.3 *Possible answer:*

At the airport, follow the signs to the train station. Buy a ticket to (name of town). There are trains every hour. At (name of town) station, take a number 5 bus. The bus stop is just outside the train station. Get off the bus at the hospital, cross the street, and take the first street on the left. My house is on the corner, with a red door.

41.4

Across	Down
3. platform	1. gas
7. helicopter	2. motorcycle
9. bus	4. schedule
	5. map
	6. train
	8. taxi

Crossword grid:

```
      ¹G          ²M
³P  L   A   T   F   O   R   M
          S               T
      ⁴S              ⁵M              ⁶T
       C              R    A
⁷H  E   L   I   C   O   P  ⁸T   E  ⁶T... R
       E              Y    A          A
       D              C    X          I
⁹B  U   S             L    I          N
       L              E
       E
```

Unit 42

42.1   1. a   2. b   3. d   4. c

42.2   *Possible answers:*

No smoking: in public places (e.g., restaurant, theater, government offices, store, elevator)

Entrance and Exit – theater, museum, meeting hall, etc.

Exit – airport, theater, stadium, parking garage, etc.

Caution: Wet floor – in a public restroom (toilet)

Pay here – in a store or restaurant

Out of order – on a public phone, on a vending machine, on a photocopier, etc.

Push and Pull – on doors in public places (e.g., store, train station, museum)

Sale – on a store window, on a display inside a store

Open and Closed – on the door of a store, restaurant, or museum

Keep off the grass - in some parks, on the lawn (grass) outside a public building

Men/Women *or* Gentlemen/Ladies – in a restaurant, airport, theater, park, etc.

Restrooms – Same as Men/Women

42.3   2. No   3. No   4. A   5. B   6. Yes, if the discounts are large enough!

42.4   *Suggested answers:*

Information	**Instructions**
Entrance and Exit	No smoking
Caution: Wet floor	Pay here
Out of order	Push and Pull
Sale	Keep off the grass.
Open and Closed	
Men/Women, Gentlemen/Ladies, Restrooms	

Unit 43

43.1   2. potatoes   4. meat   6. fast food / junk food
        3. pasta   5. desserts

43.2

Fruits	Vegetables
pineapple	green bean
grapes	carrot
orange	onion
banana	garlic
pear	mushroom

Possible additions:

apple	peas
strawberry	potato
kiwi	lettuce
peach	celery

43.3
1. banana   3. potatoes   5. apple
2. tomatoes   4. strawberries

43.4

Unit 44

44.1
2. yes
3. yes
4. no (The freezer is *colder* than the refrigerator.)
5. yes
6. no (A dishtowel makes plates *dry*.)

44.2   *Possible questions:*
1. Where can I find the coffee?
   Where's the tea?
2. Where's the pot?
   Where's the frying pan?
3. Where should I put this mug?
4. Can I help with the dishes?

44.3   *Possible answers:*
2. tea, a teapot, a cup, a spoon
3. an egg, a frying pan, butter or oil, a stove
4. a plate or bowl, a knife and fork, or a spoon, or chopsticks
5. water and a glass, or a cup, or a mug
6. a microwave

44.4
1. a microwave   3. ice   5. milk
2. a pot   4. a coffeemaker   6. a mug

Unit 45

45.1
2. closet
3. dresser / chest of drawers
4. night table / nightstand
5. alarm clock
6. table lamp
7. mirror
8. pajamas
9. pillow

45.2 *Possible answers:*

toothpaste, hairbrush, comb, pajamas or nightgown, shampoo

45.3
2. Aya is washing her face.
3. Mr. and Mrs. Park are having/eating breakfast.
4. Mr. Park is taking a bath.
5. James is getting dressed.
6. Antonio is turning off the light.   *or*   Antonio is going to bed.

45.4 *Possible answers:*

bath, shower, toilet, toilet paper, sink, soap, shampoo, towels, toothbrush, toothpaste, mirror, medicine cabinet/chest, shelf

45.5 *Possible answer:*

In my bedroom there is a big bed. There is a closet on the right side of the room. The closet door has a mirror on it. I have a night table with a lamp and an alarm clock on it. There is a dresser beside the window. The dresser has five drawers in it.

45.6 *Possible answer:*

I usually go to bed at 10 p.m. I get undressed and take a bath. I am usually tired, but I always read for a while. I turn off the light after ten minutes. I fall asleep quickly. I wake up before my alarm clock rings, but I don't get out of bed. I get up when my alarm clock rings. I wash my face, brush my teeth, and get dressed. I go to the kitchen for breakfast.

Unit 46

46.1 *Suggested answers:*
2. a sofa/couch
3. a coffee table, an end table
4. a picture
5. a light switch
6. a CD player, a stereo, a tape player, a radio
7. a carpet

46.2
1. (c) a sofa
2. (b) switch on the reading lamp
3. (a) use the remote control

46.3
2. in; on   3. near   4. against   5. in . . . of

46.4 *Possible answer:*

In my living room there is a table, a TV, a desk, a sofa, and two armchairs. The TV is near the window, and the sofa is against the wall. The table is in the middle of the room. The walls are white, and there are some pictures on them. I like to relax in the living room. In the evening I watch TV there or listen to music.

46.5

Unit 47

47.1 *Suggested answers:*

2. A doctor works in a hospital (or a clinic, or a doctor's office).
3. A waiter works in a restaurant (or a cafe).
4. A secretary works in an office.
5. A salesclerk works in a store.
6. A farmer works on a farm.

47.2 1. lawyer 2. mechanic 3. taxi driver 4. secretary 5. farmer 6. nurse

47.3 *Possible answers:*

1. I'm a teacher. 2. At a university. 3. Yes, very interesting.

47.4

Across	*Down*
1. bus driver	1. doctor
2. teacher	2. waiter
3. writer	3. nurse

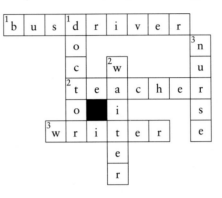

Unit 48

48.1

2. d	5. b	8. a
3. g	6. i	9. h
4. f	7. e	

48.2 *Possible answers:*

My three favorite subjects are physical education, English, and art. I don't like physics, chemistry, and math.

48.3 notebook, cassette, tape recorder / tape player, pencil, eraser, ruler, paper clips, pen, pencil sharpener, thumbtacks

48.4 *Possible answers:*

a tape recorder and some cassettes, notebooks, pens, paper clips, pencils, a chalkboard, chalk, an eraser, and a pencil sharpener

48.5

2. did	6. take	10. fails
3. passed	7. take	11. give
4. studying *or* taking	8. passes	
5. taking	9. get (*also*: receive)	

Unit 49

49.1 *Possible answers:*

answering machine, telephone, cell phone, letters, envelopes, stamps, computer, monitor, mouse, keyboard

49.2   2. public telephone / pay phone   5. mouse   8. mailbox
    3. cell phone   6. address   9. monitor
    4. stamp   7. envelope

49.3   1. This   2. speak   3. sorry   4. take (*also:* give him)   5. call (him)

49.5   *Possible answers:*
    2. E-mail is often cheapest (if you have the equipment).
    3. I've sent and received them all.
    4. Talking on the telephone because I like to talk to my friends.
    5. I use e-mail most often for business.

Unit 50

50.1   1. on   2. local   3. time (*also:* vacation)   4. by

50.2   1. a package tour   3. a winter vacation
    2. a bus tour   4. camping   *or*   going camping

50.3   *Possible answers:*
    1. A car is usually faster.
    2. Traveling by car is usually cheaper, especially for a family.
    3. You can take more luggage on a ferry.
    4. You can see more from a car, in most cases.

50.4   2. luggage   3. passport   4. phrase book   5. camera   6. tickets

50.5   1. traveler's checks   2. a visa   3. postcards   4. nightlife

Unit 51

51.1   1. pharmacy   3. hardware store   5. gift shop
    2. toy store   4. newsstand   6. bakery

51.2   2. the hairdresser   5. a bookstore
    3. the post office   6. a department store (*also:* a supermarket)
    4. a gift shop

51.3   1. 4th   4. basement   7. main   10. 4th
    2. main   5. 2nd   8. 3rd   11. main
    3. 5th   6. basement   9. 3rd   12. 3rd

51.4   2. cash   4. a credit card   6. the cashier / cash register
    3. a hairdresser/hairstylist   5. the basement   7. a receipt

51.5   1. cost   2. pay   3. bag / shopping bag

Unit 52

52.1   2. nonsmoking   5. coffeemaker   8. elevator
    3. TV/television   6. floor   9. luggage (*also:* bags)
    4. telephone/phone   7. (room) key

52.2   2. a   3. h   4. f   5. b   6. g   7. c   8. e

52.3   *Possible answers:*

1. From $50 to $300 per night, depending on the quality of the hotel.
2. 1
3. Varies by country.
4. Because if you lose them or if they are stolen, you can get your money back.

52.4   *Possible answers:*

Can I have a wake-up call, please?
Can I have room service, please?
Can I book/reserve a room for next week, please?
Can I have a double room for tonight, please?
Can I have my bill, please?
Can I have a hair dryer, please?

Unit 53

53.1   *Possible answers:*

2. a restaurant   3. a fast-food restaurant or a coffee shop   4. a cafe

53.2   *Possible answers:*

cafe – Corner Cafe
restaurant – The Second Street Grill
coffee shop – Athens Coffee Shop
deli – the New York Stage Deli
fast-food restaurant – Burger King

53.3   *Possible answers:*

1. I'd choose tomato soup, chicken salad, and chocolate ice cream.
2. A vegetarian might choose fried mushrooms; tomato or onion soup; a cheese omelet, or a plain omelet, or the pasta primavera; a green salad; and any of the beverages and desserts.
3. Four dishes made with chicken are chicken wings, chicken soup, grilled chicken breast, and chicken salad.
4. cola

53.4   2. omelet   3. salad   4. potatoes   5. ice cream   6. steak

53.5

WAITER:	Are you ready **to** order?
CUSTOMER:	Yes. **I'd like** the vegetable soup and a hamburger, please.
WAITER:	**How** would you like your hamburger? Rare, medium, or **well-done**?
CUSTOMER:	Medium.
WAITER:	Anything to drink?
CUSTOMER:	**An** iced tea, please.

Unit 54

54.1   2. sailing   3. tennis   4. soccer   5. ice-skating   6. swimming

54.2   1. tennis   3. baseball   5. golf
         2. basketball   4. table tennis (Ping-Pong)   6. skiing

54.3 *Suggested answers:*
2. What's your favorite sport?
3. Do you play any sports?
4. go swimming? / like swimming? / swim?

Unit 55

55.1
2. science fiction   4. action   6. romance   8. musical
3. horror   5. cartoon/animated   7. crime/detective

55.2

```
        C R I M E
      H O R R O R
      C O M E D Y
          A C T I O N
  S C I E N C E   F I C T I O N
      W E S T E R N
      M U S I C A L
          C A R T O O N
```

55.3 *Suggested answers:*
1. to (the)   3. played   5. movie stars
2. watched (*also:* saw *or* rented)   4. in   6. director

55.4 *Possible answers:*
1. *Star Wars, Star Trek, Alien,* etc.
2. Harrison Ford, Julia Roberts, Cameron Diaz, Antonio Banderas, Jackie Chan, etc.
3. Yes, I love them.   *or*   No, they're boring.
   Dick Tracy is one example.
4. Yes, if I'm not alone.

Unit 56

56.1 *Suggested answers:*
1. She's watching TV.   5. She's using the Internet. / She's on the
2. He's gardening.   Internet. / She's using a computer.
3. He's reading the newspaper.   6. He's listening to music.
4. She's cooking.

56.2
2. talk   4. have/invite   6. watch   8. grows
3. take   5. play   7. see/watch

56.3 *Possible answers:*
1. We talk or have a meal, or we listen to music, etc.
2. My best friend sometimes stays over. / My cousins sometimes stay over.
3. I like novels, and I read the newspaper every day.
4. I call them almost every day, sometimes a few times a day.

56.4 *Possible answers for a young person who likes technology:*

⟵————————————————————————————⟶

Most interesting						*Most boring*
using the Internet	watching videos	listening to music	reading	doing nothing	cooking	gardening

Unit 57

57.1 2. a (bank) robber   3. a shoplifter   4. a burglar   5. a (jewel) thief

57.2 2. vandals   4. fine   6. burglaries
3. speeding   5. innocent   7. hacker

57.3 *Possible answers:*
1. a   2. b   3. a   4. i   5. c   6. h

57.4 *Possible answers:*

$\longrightarrow$

$\longleftarrow$

Most serious   *Least serious*
robbery   burglary   theft   speeding   hacking   shoplifting   vandalism

Unit 58

58.1 2. documentary (*also:* program)   4. nature   6. Internet
3. fashion   5. teen   7. comic books / comics

58.2 1. e   2. d   3. b   4. a   5. c

58.3 1. c   2. a   3. d   4. b

58.4 2. a journalist   4. a comic book / a comic
3. an evening (news)paper   5. a documentary

58.5 *Possible answers:*
1. I always read a morning newspaper.
2. I get 30 channels.
3. I watch two or three hours every day.
4. I like documentaries and movies on TV. I like to listen to talk shows and music on the radio.

Unit 59

59.1 2. She has too much work.   6. The room is messy.
3. Her computer crashed.   7. The phone is out of order. /
4. His hand is cut.   The phone isn't working.
5. The cup is broken.   8. He is late for work.

59.2 *Possible answers:*
2. finger/hand/knees   5. camera/microwave/radio
3. room/desk/hair   6. TV / washing machine / hair dryer
4. school / an appointment / work

59.3 *Possible answers:*

Big problems
a computer crash
a broken washing machine
lost keys
an argument with a friend
late for work
too much work
a coffeemaker that isn't working

Small problems
a TV that doesn't work
a messy bedroom
a cut finger
dying plants
a photocopier that is out of order
a coworker in a bad mood

59.4 *Possible answers:*

too much work – get an assistant
a co-worker in a bad mood – ignore it
a crashed computer – call a technician
a photocopier that is out of order – repair the photocopier
a coffeemaker that isn't working – drink water

59.5 *Possible answers:*

My CD player doesn't work.
My brother lost his credit card.
My friend broke a glass.

Unit 60

60.1
2. car crash
3. flood
4. war
5. earthquake
6. forest fire
7. hurricane
8. traffic jam
9. snowstorm

60.2 *Possible answers:*

snowstorm – Canada
forest fire – Australia
earthquake – Turkey
flood – Bangladesh

60.3 *Possible answers:*

We have poor people in big cities, hungry people in big cities, homeless people in the south, unemployed people in the north, too many people in the capital, traffic jams in big cities, car crashes on main roads, and strikes in some factories. Fortunately, we don't have any wars.

60.4 *Possible answers:*

earthquake, car crash – things get smashed
forest fire, pollution, traffic jams – they make the environment dirty
poor, unemployed, hungry, and homeless people – too many people
strike, war – problems caused by government and politics

60.5
2. strike
3. War
4. crash (also: accident)
5. earthquakes; snowstorms
6. homeless